W9-CCV-158

Southern Sr. High Media Center
Harwood, Maryland 20776

36031300435476 2

The Warsaw Ghetto Uprising

Elaine Landau

A TIMESTOP BOOK

new
Discovery
B·O·O·K·S

New York

Maxwell Macmillan Canada
Toronto

Maxwell Macmillan International
New York Oxford Singapore Sydney

FOR SUSAN GRAVER

Designer: Deborah Fillion
Photos courtesy of Yad-Vashem, Jerusalem

Copyright © 1992 by Elaine Landau

All rights reserved. No part of this book may be reproduced or transmitted in any form or by any means, electronic or mechanical, including photocopying, recording, or by any information storage and retrieval system, without permission in writing from the Publisher.

New Discovery Books
Macmillan Publishing Company
866 Third Avenue
New York, NY 10022

Maxwell Macmillan Canada, Inc.
1200 Eglinton Avenue East
Suite 200
Don Mills, Ontario M3C 3N1

Macmillan Publishing Company is part of the Maxwell Communication Group of Companies.

First edition

Printed in the United States of America

10 9 8 7 6 5 4 3 2 1

Library of Congress Cataloging-in-Publication Data

Landau, Elaine.
  The Warsaw ghetto uprising / by Elaine Landau.
     p.   cm.
  Includes bibliographical references (p.   ) and index.
  Summary: Describes life in the section of Warsaw where Polish Jews were confined by the Nazis in the early 1940s, focusing on the final days of fighting prior to the destruction of the ghetto in 1943.
  ISBN 0-02-751392-0
  1. Warsaw (Poland)—History—Uprising of 1943—Juvenile literature. 2. Jews—Poland—Warsaw—Persecutions—Juvenile literature. 3. Holocaust, Jewish (1939-1945)—Poland—Warsaw—Juvenile literature. 4. Warsaw (Poland)—Ethnic relations—Juvenile literature. [1. Warsaw (Poland)—History—Uprising of 1943. 2. Jews—Poland—Warsaw—Persecutions. 3. Holocaust, Jewish (1939-1945)—Poland—Warsaw. 4. Poland—History—Occupation, 1939-1945. 5. World War, 1939-1945—Jews.] I. Title.
DS135.P62W285 1992
940.53'18'094386—dc20   92-15851

CONTENTS

Prologue   In the Beginning   5

Chapter 1   The Early Days   9

Chapter 2   Fortifying the Ghetto   23

Chapter 3   Trouble Nears   37

Chapter 4   The Beginning of the End   49

Chapter 5   The Onslaught   67

Chapter 6   The Battle Continues   79

Chapter 7   The Burning Ghetto   91

Chapter 8   Hope and Sorrow   99

Chapter 9   The Last Stages   109

Chapter 10   A Rebellion Trampled   119

Epilogue   The Rebellion's End   133

              Source Notes   137

              For Further Reading   139

              Index   141

A crowded street in Warsaw's Jewish ghetto

PROLOGUE

In the Beginning

B y the late 1930s Warsaw, Poland's capital, was considered one of Europe's most exciting cities. Having grown from a small walled town during the Middle Ages, Warsaw eventually emerged as a city of magnificent palatial homes that mingled with more modest dwellings and even slums. Although the city bustled with industry and commerce, Warsaw was also an important art and intellectual center. A seemingly magnetic draw for artists, actors, writers, and thinkers, Warsaw was known for its cultural chic. On any summer day, fashionable Warsaw residents could be seen enjoying coffee and conversation in one of the city's many outdoor cafés or strolling down a historic promenade.

That was Warsaw *before* the war. In September 1939 Nazi forces invaded Poland while attempting to fulfill Hitler's dream of acquiring a substantial German empire. More than 80 percent of the city was eventually destroyed during that vicious military encounter.[1] By the end of the war much of Warsaw's landscape was marred by burned-out residences and churches, smashed bridges, and overturned streetcars.

Although the lives of most Polish citizens were dramatically altered during the German takeover, perhaps none experienced the Nazi conquerors' cunning and brutality as strongly as the nation's Jewish population. Historical estimates indicate that Jews were present in Poland since 890, gathering there to escape the persecution they had experienced in neighboring areas. These early settlers multiplied and before long Poland's Jewish community significantly expanded. Tending to dwell in urban areas, a substantial number of Jews resided in Warsaw.

While through the centuries Jews frequently assisted Poles in fending off invading foreign regimes, to a large extent they remained apart from the Christian majority. Polish Jews persistently clung to their Yiddish language and distinctively different clothing and traditions. Although they were hardworking and therefore useful to Poland's economy, the country's Jews had never been well liked or fully accepted. For the most part, they were poor and oppressed, and at times forced to endure the bitter sting of sporadic anti-Semitic assaults.

As might be expected there was little local resistance to the Nazis' blatant persecution of Polish Jews following Hitler's invasion. The Germans were swift and ruthless in their efforts to resolve what they'd mildly dubbed "the Jewish question." By October 1940 nearly half a million Jews, about a third of Warsaw's total population, were barricaded into a large walled-in slum area of the city known as the ghetto. It was the first major step in the annihilation of these people.

The Nazis frequently segregated Jews in ghettos as a transitional measure until they were able to entirely "cleanse" a city of them. These sealed-off areas proved to be effective instruments for genocide. Warehoused in ghettos, the Jews were kept out of sight before they were shipped off to labor camps or extermination centers. Isolating them from the city's Christian population served to discourage any sympathy for this severely oppressed minority.

Yet despite the Third Reich's well-designed and well-implemented plan for their slaughter, Warsaw Jews fought back. A group of largely young people, some in their teens, others in their early twenties, stood together to reject death on the Nazis' terms. Even in the face of insurmountable odds, they proved to be remarkably resourceful in thwarting their enemy. "We fought not only for our lives," one rebel leader recalled. "We fought for life in dignity and freedom." This is their story.

A homeless mother and her children
sleep on the street in the ghetto.

CHAPTER 1

The Early Days

The Warsaw ghetto encompassed an expanse of nearly 1,000 acres in the most run-down part of the city. While poor Warsaw Christians and Jews had previously occupied this area jointly, the Christians had moved into superior dwellings seized by the Nazis from affluent Jews in other parts of Warsaw. The hammerhead-shaped ghetto was deliberately segregated from the rest of the city by a ten-foot wall that stretched eleven miles to encircle the entire area. The wall was topped with both barbed wire and layers of broken glass to discourage escape attempts. Jews were not permitted to either enter or leave the ghetto without a special pass.

As time passed, the Nazis managed to divide the ghetto's interior into three distinct parts. The "shop section," called the productive ghetto, was mainly composed of businesses owned by Germans and staffed by Jews who were paid almost nothing for their labor. Here stone walls encircled each factory as well as the workers' living quarters. A second ghetto section consisted of several German brush-making factories. Situated on a single block, these facilities turned out different types of brushes for the German army. The third area was known as the central ghetto. The central ghetto contained only a few factories and many apartment buildings in which the majority of the Jews lived. The Judenrat headquarters were also established there. *Judenrat* was the name given to the Jewish councils established by the Nazis in the various countries they invaded. Nazi demands were frequently channeled to the Jewish population through the Judenrat.

Large-scale overcrowding was part of the Nazi plan to devastate the ghetto. The region's long blocks of tenement buildings teemed with an overwhelming number of newly arrived Jews, whom the Nazis had crowded into this restricted zone. In addition to Warsaw's Jews, thousands of Polish Jews from nearby towns and villages were sent to the Warsaw ghetto. Both practicing Jews and Poles of Jewish origin—individuals who had either previously converted to Christianity or had always considered themselves Christians, but were known to have had a Jewish grandparent—were forced to live there.

Nearly every day, more people were wedged into the limited available space. Often thirteen or more people might occupy a single room; frequently their overflow spilled out into the stairways and courtyards adjoining the buildings. In ghetto areas where residents occupied empty warehouses alongside factories, thousands of people took up almost every inch of floor space.

But dense overcrowding was just a small part of what the Nazis would force the ghetto Jews to endure. Survival was purposely made extremely difficult for them. Residents were allotted a daily food ration of about three hundred calories—

just a fraction of what is needed to sustain a human being. They were expected to get by with only a piece of bread, which usually contained a fair amount of sawdust or potato peel, a bite or two of groats, and little more than a swallow of condensed milk. Occasionally, some might secure an ounce or two of sugar.

Before long, the Nazis' desired effects became apparent. Weak, skeletonlike figures with jaundiced, swollen faces and abdomens were seen throughout the ghetto. The Nazis made certain that there were few available relief routes for Warsaw's Jews. Although sickness and diseases such as typhoid, typhus, and paratyphoid were rampant in the ghetto due to overcrowding and poor sanitation, residents were left without drugs or medical supplies of any kind.

Three or four people might share one lice-infested mattress in an unstaffed hospital, praying for help that never came. To speedily rid the ghetto of those who were least useful to them, the Nazis denied any type of medical attention to individuals under three or over forty-five years of age. Under these conditions, Warsaw Jews perished at an annual rate of nearly fifty thousand.

The stench of death filled the ghetto as people dying of disease and starvation made their way out to the street to beg passersby for food scraps. Many did not have the strength to make it back into the buildings and died outdoors. Their corpses were soon joined by scores of other bodies, which were covered with old newspapers and magazines and left on the curb to be hauled off to a mass grave outside the ghetto.

Yet, amazingly, even under these circumstances, Warsaw Jews were determined to survive. They tried to thwart the Nazis' systematic debilitation process by organizing to bring about change.

Since food was a priority, a great deal of effort centered on feeding ghetto residents. Each building established committees to identify those in most dire need and to initiate possible remedies. The committees proved to be exceedingly resourceful. Before long, vegetable gardens were spotted growing on building rooftops and terraces. These were supplemented by communal soup kitchens formed by the residents.

Perhaps the Warsaw Jews' most crucial survival links were the trade alliances they managed to establish with the gentile world beyond the ghetto walls. Although the Nazis had tried to confiscate everything of value the Jews owned, many families had been able to hide various expensive objects by burying them in their backyards or temporarily leaving them with trusted Christian friends or neighbors. Now they found that their lives often depended on such items as gemstones and gold jewelry, furs, silver candlesticks, and highly valued coins. Some ghetto Jews also secured funds by working in the ghetto factories owned by German businessmen. Although they were only paid a small fraction of what they should have earned, their meager wages helped them fend off starvation.

The Jewish-gentile barter system that took root in the ghetto depended on an unusually effective smuggling ring. The range of ghetto smugglers involved in the ongoing operation was extremely diverse. Some of the amateur smugglers were children small enough to crawl through the ghetto's sewer pipes or slip through openings in walls without being detected by the guards posted at the ghetto's fourteen entrances. Once outside, they'd trade whatever valuables or money their families had for a handful of food.

On a more intensive level, both Jewish and Christian professional smugglers ran a sophisticated operation that fre-

German guards search children
caught smuggling food.

quently entailed bribing guards, police, and Nazi soldiers. For predetermined and often exorbitant sums, seemingly uninvolved workers entered the ghetto, bringing in food supplies for the residents: Sanitation workers returned garbage drums to the ghetto filled with a variety of foods; wagons and hearses carrying out the dead simultaneously delivered needed supplies.

The smugglers made good use of the ghetto's architecture and design whenever possible. Milk was poured into a pipe on the gentile side of the ghetto wall and flowed out the opposite end into waiting buckets. Temporary portable ramps were even constructed so that live cattle and oxen could be herded over the ghetto wall to be butchered for food.

Yet many ghetto residents had mixed feelings about the smugglers living among them. These individuals, who were generally not very well liked, were said to be extremely uncharitable. They'd callously ignore the pleas of starving children in the street while on their way to collect money owed them from those with financial resources. Many smugglers lived comfortably in the ghetto off the last dollars of hungry, desperate people, frequently enjoying liquor and an abundance of food that they'd hoarded for themselves. Nevertheless, these individuals were essential to the continuance of Warsaw's Jewish community.

Besides devising a superior smuggling network, Warsaw Jews were extremely enterprising in other ways. They would frequently gather leftover scraps and remnants from German factories in the ghetto to fashion sweaters, coats, and pants. Discarded broom bristles and feathers were recycled into brushes and pillow stuffings. Residents even made suitcases out of old book-ledger covers.

Despite the high level of deprivation they had to contend

with, many ghetto residents still longed to enrich their minds and spirits. Although the ghetto Jews had been forbidden to operate schools, young people were secretly taught by ghetto youth and welfare organizations in attics, basements, and an assortment of other well-hidden places. Even Yiddish theater troupes and cultural organizations tried to remain active in the ghetto.

Suffering and death were still undeniable features of ghetto life, yet through their ingenuity and determination, a large number of Warsaw Jews lived considerably longer than the Nazis had intended. Enraged at how their victims clung to life, the Germans grew even more anxious to diminish ghetto morale. By the spring of 1942, they relied on the sadistic brutality of two SS men—Heinrich Klaustermeyer and Josef Blosche—to terrorize Warsaw's Jews. The well-armed pair would leisurely stroll down ghetto streets, randomly shooting at babies in strollers or at any figure that might appear in a doorway or window.

Young Jewish girls were particularly at risk, since they were frequently raped and killed, but anyone could be singled out to die at either man's whim. At times when they were tired of shooting Jews, the men might force someone on the street to stop and drink a cup of poison.

Unfortunately, Klaustermeyer and Blosche were not the only Nazis who engaged in this type of brutality. In varying degrees, other SS members made the indiscriminate torture and murder of Jews a common Nazi pastime. As one ghetto resident who kept a diary of his Warsaw experiences wrote:

When a German appears in the streets of the ghetto, everyone crosses over to the opposite sidewalk, just as one keeps his distance from a beast of prey. And this, as a matter of fact, is not cowardice. When a Nazi meets a Jew, the outcome is harm, and if you escape your Jewish obligation of death by accepting a blow from a stick or a whiplash you are among the fortunate. Sometimes the Nazis invite you to follow them— then your life is [really] in danger. . . . This is a basic rule: Every Nazi is a killer by nature, and when he is in Jewish surroundings, he spreads death and destruction.[1]

Between October 1940 and July 1942, nearly 100,000 Warsaw ghetto residents perished as a result of their inhumane living conditions, but the Nazis were still dissatisfied with what they perceived as the too-slow deterioration of the community. Starvation had not obliterated Warsaw Jewry as a Nazi official had predicted when he said, "The Jews will die from hunger and destitution and a cemetery will remain of the Jewish question." The SS terror tactics had been insufficient as well.

The Nazis decided that increasingly deliberate and measurable methods needed to be put into effect. Before long, Warsaw ghetto residents began to hear rumors about resettlement. Some believed that the entire ghetto was to be uprooted and sent to labor camps in various parts of Poland. There were also more disturbing stories indicating that these labor camps were actually annihilation centers from which they were not expected to leave.

Many of the residents initially refused to believe that such large-scale atrocities could be plotted and carried out against European Jews. They argued that some of the Jews were working in German-owned ghetto shops producing direly needed supplies for Germany's war effort. It was difficult for them to imagine that the entire ghetto could be destroyed, but that was precisely the Nazis' plan.

On July 22, 1942, the once-whispered-about nightmare finally came to pass. Posters and announcements went out proclaiming the upcoming resettlement. Within hours, a train composed of a string of cattle cars pulled into the northern end of the ghetto to carry residents to camps where they might be either promptly gassed or slowly worked to death.

Each day, thousands of Warsaw Jews were ordered to report for deportation. The parting scenes were simultaneously chaotic and sad as men, women, and children were forced into the train cars. Terrified of what their final destination might be, at the last minute many people searched for ways to save themselves.

They knew that the Germans would exempt anyone who could prove that he or she was a registered ghetto worker, so as not to drain the labor pool relied on by German industrialists with ghetto factories. Many of these factory owners had prospered from Jewish labor early on, since their shops and machinery had been confiscated from successful Jews who paid for the privilege of remaining in the establishments as managers.

They did so hoping that the Nazis would regard them as useful to the Third Reich and save them from the transports. Now that the trains were pulling out, large numbers of panic-stricken Jews hoped the same strategy would work for them. They begged the German industrialists for jobs, offering them whatever valuables they had left in exchange for the precious employment cards that would keep them off the trains.

At times, nearly everyone standing in the deportation line tightly grasped a piece of paper to prove that he or she was employed. Some of the cards were genuine, but most were

A group of Jews are deported from Warsaw to the
dreaded prison camps.

poorly executed forgeries. Before long, some individuals would be seen lying in pools of their own blood after having been severely beaten by the Nazis for wasting their time with invalid employment registrations.

Only a select number managed to evade the Nazi deportation call legally. Most boarded the train to find there was little room in which to sit down or move about during the journey. Often the passengers traveled to their destinations pressed against one another like canned sardines. Others chose not to report but instead to hide out in the ghetto, risking immediate execution if captured.

In some cases, people who clearly knew what lay ahead boarded the trains, not wanting to be left behind if their families and loved ones went. That's how it was for Janusz Korczak, the ghetto's orphanage director. When the Nazis ordered the 200 children in his care to report for deportation, he insisted on accompanying them, even though his name had not yet come up.

He carefully dressed the children in their best clothes and told them to bring their schoolbooks so that they would not fall behind in their studies while away. Then, taking a child in each hand, he instructed the others to follow quietly in line as they made their way to the deportation area. The group left the ghetto with dignity, even though Korczak knew that young children were among those immediately gassed upon arriving at the camps. It was later reported that he told the children fairy tales to calm them as he entered the death chamber with them.

Deportation was an ongoing nightmare that touched the lives of all ghetto families. Even as a young girl in the ghetto, Eva Kampinski realized that these selections could result in the loss of one's family at a moment's notice. As she described the predicament in an interview: "They took my father and my sister . . . and they took my mother the following day. . . . I believed the reports filtering back about the killing center of Treblinka [a Nazi death camp]. Of course, one always hopes and doesn't want to believe the worst, but reality had to be faced."[2]

The hideous roundups and deportations of ghetto Jews continued throughout the summer months and finally ended when the last train pulled out on September 13, 1942. During that period, approximately 300,000 Jews were taken from the ghetto. Organized efforts on the part of ghetto residents to stop the incipient carnage had not yet crystallized, although there were individual acts of sabotage against both the Nazis and those who did their bidding. These even included an attempted assassination of the ghetto police commander, Joseph Szerynski.

Szerynski, who headed the ghetto's Jewish police force, was known to follow Nazi orders zealously. He was a prime example of how a crisis sometimes brings out the worst in people. A considerable number of young men on his force were from wealthy families and therefore had the resources to buy their ways into this relatively safe position. As the police were required to meet a daily quota in rounding up Jews who had evaded deportation, they saved themselves by turning in their own people. Some even gave up their own parents, telling themselves that the old people had already enjoyed full lives.

Police Colonel Szerynski had shown himself to be particularly enthusiastic in hunting for Jews who tried to escape. Many in the ghetto swore that he was harder on these individuals than most German officers, and were anxious to be rid of him. So one evening, a ghetto freedom fighter disguised in a

The Jewish police force of the Warsaw ghetto

police uniform arrived at the colonel's home, claiming that he had an important message for him. Although he meant to kill the ghetto bully, the young man only succeeded in wounding him. However, racked with pain as a result of his injury, Szerynski took his own life several months later.

By then the ghetto had been reduced to a tenth of its former size through various Nazi atrocities. A portion of the area between the different sections, which had come to be called the wild ghetto, had deteriorated into a shambles resembling a war zone. Many of the cobblestone streets now lay covered with shattered window glass, ripped clothing remnants, and broken furniture. After deporting scores of families, the Nazis had ransacked the abandoned dwellings, taking anything of possible value and throwing what remained into the street. This section had also become filled with "illegal" Jews, including thieves, smugglers, and those who'd failed to report for deportation. Now they lived like hunted animals trying to remain one step ahead of their pursuers. Because these Jews were known as desperate individuals who would stop at nothing if threatened, even the ghetto police hesitated to enter the areas they occupied.

The reduced-sized ghetto encompassed both the illegal residents and those who had not yet been earmarked for deportation. These people were the remnants of formerly whole families. They were what remained following the Nazis' deportation and starvation efforts. Some were parentless teenagers, while others were parents who'd lost their children. Countless widows and widowers were also among those left. These individuals might have once had vastly different concerns and interests, but they had become united in their belief that the Nazis intended to kill them, and many now refused to die without a fight.

CHAPTER 2

Fortifying the Ghetto

As the Warsaw Jews prepared to defend against the upcoming Nazi onslaught, they knew that this battle would be like no other. The ghetto residents were at an obvious disadvantage. The Nazis had the element of surprise on their side—they could strike at any hour of the day or night, while the ghetto residents could at best retaliate. The Jews were also unable to move the fighting to new ground, since they were confined to a walled-in area.

The Germans' firepower was that of a well-outfitted army and included unlimited tanks, artillery, and machine guns. The Warsaw Jews eventually managed to secure some pistols, a few thousand grenades and Molotov cocktails, and a very limited number of mines, rifles, and automatic weapons.

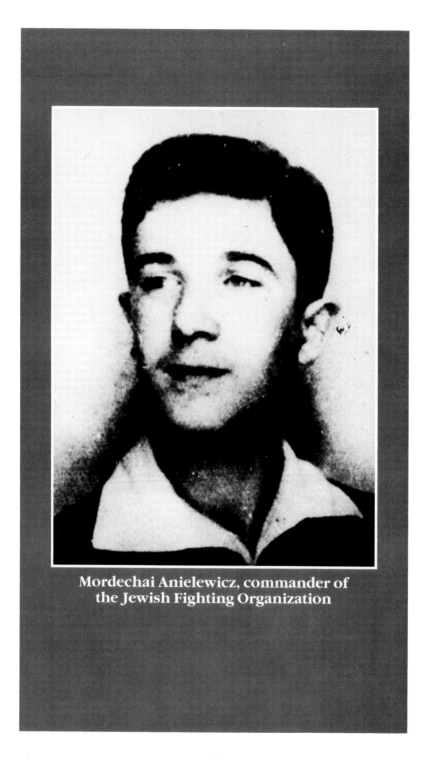

Mordechai Anielewicz, commander of
the Jewish Fighting Organization

Yet there were some undeniably important factors favoring the would-be ghetto fighters. The ghetto's construction could actually serve as a large complex maze that might assist rebels in inflicting sizable enemy casualties. By tearing down attic walls in strategic areas, the residents managed to create an ingenious network of interconnected spaces completely hidden from enemy view. The system would afford ghetto warriors opportunities to shift positions, retreat from battle, and move substantial quantities of supplies to where they were most needed.

A second factor in the ghetto residents' favor was their superior motivation. These soldiers were unlikely to surrender, since they did not wish to assist the Germans in exterminating their own people. While they knew they could never defeat the Nazis, armed resistance would at least allow them to choose how they would die.

A crucial component in the residents' resistance movement was the Jewish Fighting Organization (Zydowska Orgawizacja Bojowa, or the ZOB). There were about 800 ZOB fighters in the ghetto. Their 24-year-old commander in chief was Mordechai Anielewicz, who was frequently referred to as "Angel" due to his noble character and because his last name came from the Polish word meaning angel.

The ZOB was composed of a number of factions. Initially, Jewish members of the Communist Polish Workers' party (PPR) had been anxious to establish a ghetto resistance movement. In February 1942, its leaders met with Mordechai Anielewicz and members of a number of militant Jewish youth organizations. They decided to join together to form what was known as the Anti-Fascist Bloc. The Bloc hoped to initiate underground resistance bands, to teach ghetto rebels various fighting techniques, and to convert ghetto residents who were still unsure of the appropriate course of action.

Anxious to begin its work, the Bloc began an underground press to get the word out. Unfortunately, Nazi retaliation against the Bloc's activities began shortly thereafter. In April 1942, 52 highly respected ghetto Jews were rounded up and murdered. Sadly, the reprisal killings didn't end with these deaths. Ghetto residents lived in continual fear as nearly every day more Jews were randomly murdered as a warning to the Bloc to cease its activities. And when the Germans captured a number of PPR leaders that following month, the Anti-Fascist Bloc disintegrated.

Nevertheless, along with numerous others, Mordechai Anielewicz remained determined to organize a ghetto revolt. At that point, several ghetto youth groups, the remaining PPR members, and the Bund (the Hebrew Social Democratic party—the party of most of Poland's Jewish workers and arti-sans) pooled their energy and resources to stage an armed ghetto rebellion. This was how the ZOB was formed—a fighting force largely composed of men and women between 18 and 20 who chose Mordechai Anielewicz as their leader.

Anielewicz was an ideal commander for the task at hand. He was a Polish Jew who had grown up in an impoverished, high-crime district of Warsaw. Mordechai learned that, to survive, a Jew might always have to fight in one way or another. Although Anielewicz generally got along well with the neighborhood gentiles, he would readily fight anyone who picked on Jews or resorted to anti-Semitic name-calling.

As Anielewicz grew older, these confrontations became increasingly frequent and brutal. The boy often returned from school with a bloody nose, blackened eyes, and torn clothes. On some occasions he'd enlist the help of his younger brother in fighting the Christian boys who taunted and humiliated

Jewish youths. In time he organized a group of Jewish teens to come to the defense of any Jew targeted by neighborhood gentiles.

As an adult, Mordechai Anielewicz once again assumed a leadership role as he devised the Warsaw ghetto's underground defense movement. He believed that it was imperative for Jews to rise up against Nazi oppression. As the young commander in chief implored those attending a secret meeting of the group: "The most difficult struggle of all is the one within ourselves. Let us not get accustomed to these conditions. The one who adjusts ceases to discriminate between good and evil. He becomes a slave in body and soul. Whatever may happen to you, remember always: Don't adjust! Revolt against the reality."[1]

Any ghetto residents who'd been reluctant to support the rebels were forced to heed Anielewicz's warning when on January 18, 1943, the Nazis initiated another surprise action in the ghetto. This time the ZOB fought back, although initially it seemed unlikely that they would succeed. At the time, the group had secured only a handful of pistols, some grenades, and the ingredients for a number of Molotov cocktails.

Yet the ZOB fighters joined the line of terrified Jews reporting for deportation, and, as planned, one of the fighters hurled a grenade at an unsuspecting German guard. The Jews in tow had a chance to disperse, and the fighting began. The rebels used their limited weapon supply, along with rocks, boards, and their fists, to fight the Nazis.

There were other examples of the rebels' quick thinking and bravery. Among the heroes of the January 1943 resistance was a twenty-year-old ZOB commander named Zachariah Artsein. After locating what they thought might be ZOB headquarters, all the Nazis found was young Artsein sitting in an easy chair, calmly reading a book. Not perceiving this young person as a threat, they proceeded to the apartment's interior, where the other fighters were hiding. But Artsein jumped up and shot the Nazis in the back before they realized what was happening.

Seconds later, the other ZOB fighters emerged to confront the additional German soldiers waiting in the hallway. The rebel group then went to another building, which the Nazis also invaded. This time, Artsein came out of a room with his hands held high in the air. Thinking he was alone and unarmed, the Germans were again caught off guard when the others came out firing. Several enemy soldiers were killed, and the rest fled from the building.

Astonished by the Jews' response, the Germans retreated after four days of fighting. Yet the Warsaw Jews knew that the Nazis would be back, and they began to fortify themselves for what was certain to be a life-or-death battle.

As many of the ghetto residents were either too old, too young, or too ill to attack the Nazis, they hoped to evade capture by making it as difficult as possible for the Germans to find them. To remain safely hidden within the ghetto, they secretly constructed a vast array of bunkers throughout the area. By digging out both large and small portions of the ground, ghetto residents fashioned subterranean hideaways in a variety of sizes. One bunker, which was actually an enlarged cellar beneath a building, could accommodate nearly 100 people. Such makeshift dwellings could be relied on to effectively conceal their occupants for prolonged periods.

Residents who could afford to stock their bunkers with sufficient amounts of nonperishable food to last for months on end did so. An assortment of eating utensils and books to read were usually kept in the bunkers as well. Jews realized that, in the event of a surprise Nazi attack, they would have to head for their hideouts quickly—without having time to collect what they would need. Whenever possible, the bunkers were equipped with electricity diverted from a grid running through the ghetto. Well-disguised ventilation openings ensured a steady airflow into these windowless underground worlds.

Generally, only those people directly involved in a bunker's construction or use knew of its whereabouts. Otherwise any ghetto informer could betray those inside to save him- or herself—even the most ardent rebel might weaken during one of the Nazis' infamous torture sessions.

While most ghetto families made certain that their bunkers stood ready for occupancy, from the beginning Mordechai Anielewicz decided against building bunkers for the ZOB forces. The young commander in chief feared that having such well-secluded hideaways might lessen the rebels' will to fight to the end. However, he still arranged for temporary shelter for the fighters in an oversized bunker; he also stationed auxiliary rebel squads there.

Fortifying the ZOB fighters with the necessary ammunition and supplies for what lay ahead was a nearly impossible task. Initially, the undertaking had largely been attended to by a blond, blue-eyed, Aryan-looking Jew named Arie Wilner. Wilner had passed as a Pole while living in the gentile section of Warsaw, where he'd tried to establish the contacts crucial to the ZOB's success. Arie's appearance made the loyal ZOB member especially well suited for his assignment. Christian Poles willing to assist the Jews felt comfortable around him, since they were certain that his appearance would never reveal his true identity.

Wilner was extremely interested in obtaining arms from

Arie Wilner, a leader in
the resistance movement

the Home Army (Armia Krajowa)—an underground military unit working to reinstate the conquered Polish government, which had fled to London following the Nazi invasion. After Wilner met with Home Army representatives in August 1942, a second secret meeting was held in November of the same year. Both times, Arie Wilner stressed that funding wasn't as important to the ZOB as securing actual guns, ammunition, grenades, and various types of explosives that could be used against the Nazis. He also emphasized that they needed military experts to train fighters and to offer advice on constructing "invisible" bunkers.

The Polish officers he met with promised to do all they could, but the young ZOB agent seriously doubted that much assistance would be forthcoming from what some in the ghetto had hoped would be their salvation. At their August meeting, Wilner had actively urged the Home Army to disrupt the ongoing deportations of Jews to the death camps. He felt this was not an unreasonable request, since only a minimal number of Nazi guards were assigned to the trains. But the Home Army refused, arguing that the danger to its forces was too great.

Yet Arie Wilner, along with numerous Warsaw Jews, suspected that the Home Army's motives for not acting were more sinister. While some Polish underground fighters wanted to save the Jews, many of those in command did not wish to expend their resources to halt the Nazis' Jewish extermination program. Some feared becoming prematurely involved in an escalating conflict, while many of these Poles were reluctant to risk their lives for a disliked minority.

Their feelings were apparent at a secret Home Army meeting prior to the group's first rendezvous with Wilner. The Home Army's field commander had argued in favor of assisting the Jews, since he felt that after the Nazis annihilated the ghetto population they would destroy the Christian Poles. But others at the meeting contended that if world powers such as the United States and England hadn't been able or willing to end the blatant atrocities against Jews in other nations, their small organization was under no obligation to do so in Poland. They noted that the British government had even refused to broadcast any information about the Warsaw deportations, claiming that there wasn't substantial evidence to support the reports. A number of Home Army officers also expressed the fear that if a ghetto uprising were to spread to Warsaw's gentile district, their forces were hardly prepared to take on the massive German occupation force.

Naturally, the ZOB had hoped for a more supportive reaction from both the Allied forces and the Home Army. The ZOB representatives, including Arie Wilner, argued that the Allies needed to meet violence with violence, by bombing important German cities, while simultaneously dropping leaflets exposing the plight of Polish Jews. But the response the ZOB wanted was obviously not forthcoming.

As it turned out, the Home Army offered the ZOB only minimal assistance. The Home Army claimed that it was unable to be of more help because it was short of supplies itself. Yet a Home Army memo to the Allied forces had indicated that the group actually had the following weapons: 600 heavy machine guns; 25,000 rifles; 6,000 pistols; and 30,000 grenades.

Nevertheless, the Polish underground couldn't afford to turn its back completely on Warsaw's Jews, since it didn't wish to appear inhumane in the eyes of the Allied forces that the exiled Polish government needed to come its rescue. The Home Army had also been pressured into assisting the Jews by a small but affluent and influential group of sympathetic Christian Poles known as Zegota, or the Council for Aid to the Jews.

Although Zegota members knew they'd be shot if caught, they helped many Jews escape from the ghetto and found hiding places for them in Warsaw's gentile sector. They also collected funds, from various international sources, with which to assist Poland's Jewish population.

Despite the efforts of some well-intentioned Christian Poles, the Home Army's initial delivery of arms to the ZOB was extremely disappointing. Arie Wilner described it as "scandalous" when he was given only ten pistols. To worsen matters, ZOB members later discovered that four of the guns didn't fire properly.

The Home Army's training program for ghetto fighters also proved inadequate. While the combat training sessions had been scheduled well in advance, the Polish instructor failed to appear for the first class. He arrived at the second meeting so intoxicated that he could barely stand. By then the ZOB members had lost confidence in the Home Army's commitment to them, and the training program was abandoned.

However, the ZOB continued to pressure the Home Army for additional arms. After about two months, they were given ten more pistols, along with lengthy instructions on sabotage methods and on the making of Molotov cocktails. The timing was fortunate—obtaining the guns and instructions enabled ZOB fighters to thwart the Nazis' January 1943 Jewish deportation.

That incident had convinced Arie Wilner of his people's desperate need for weapons and ammunition. No one doubted that the Nazis would be back—it was simply a question of when. Therefore, in addition to trying to induce the Home Army to support the ghetto resistance, Wilner also began purchasing weapons on the black market, hiding them in his room. Such dealings were considered extremely risky, and even those outfitting the Polish underground were forbidden to buy arms this way. A Jewish or Home Army fighter could not afford to have black-market contacts, since Nazi informers had thoroughly infiltrated their network.

Arie Wilner had felt the weapons were worth the risk, but his decision proved to be quite costly for both himself and the ZOB. One afternoon, Gestapo agents burst into his apartment and discovered his impressive stash of arms. Wilner was immediately arrested—not because he was Jewish, but because the Nazis thought he was a Polish Home Army officer.

Panic spread throughout the Polish underground once word of Wilner's arrest reached them. Having lived in the gentile sector of the city and dealt with various members of the underground, Wilner knew numerous names and addresses that the Nazis were anxious to obtain. Certain that he'd break under torture, the Home Army immediately severed its ties with the Jewish resistance and sought new hideouts for the officials known to Wilner.

Although Arie Wilner was subjected to both severe whippings and electric torture, he refused to tell his interrogators what they wanted to know. He insisted that he had no affiliation with any organized group, but had collected the weapons in his room to avenge the murder of his parents by the Germans. The Nazis' interrogation of Wilner was brutal and prolonged. He even contemplated committing suicide in his cell to make certain that he didn't give away any secrets if the torture intensified.

But Arie Wilner never betrayed the others, although he proudly admitted to being a Jew. Wilner was slated for execution, but due to a clerical error, he was confined in a local prison. Upon learning of his whereabouts, the ZOB arranged to rescue Wilner. After attempts to bribe the police failed, the organization enlisted the assistance of a friendly Christian Pole who visited the jail, claiming that a prisoner there owed him money that he desperately needed.

A guard took pity on him and allowed the Pole to see the prisoner in order to press him for cash. Wilner, who now limped badly as a result of the torture, instantly recognized the Christian Pole and understood what his rescuer meant when he angrily warned Wilner that he'd be back later that night to collect his money: Wilner knew he was to be rescued after dark.

That evening, a band of ZOB rebels located Wilner's barracks and silently led him through their planned escape route. It was difficult for Wilner to move quickly because the soles of his feet had been left nearly raw from the torture. Yet the group managed to exit the prison compound without incident. Wilner remained hidden in his Christian rescuer's home for several days while his feet began to heal. Then he returned to the ghetto, where he was reunited with his ZOB comrades. He might have been too injured by the Nazi torturers to fight with his friends, but he was prepared to die with them when the time came.

Posing as a Pole, Yitzak Zuckerman helped
those fighting within the ghetto.

CHAPTER 3

Trouble Nears

After being discovered, Arie Wilner could not resume his duties in Warsaw's gentile district, so the ZOB's second in command, Yitzhak Zuckerman, was sent in his place. Some felt that Mordechai Anielewicz should have been Wilner's replacement, as he was known for his persuasiveness, but sending Anielewicz would have posed too great a risk. Having grown up in Warsaw and been active in numerous Jewish and political organizations, he was far more likely to be detected than the relatively obscure, blond, blue-eyed Yitzhak Zuckerman.

Young Zuckerman hesitated to leave the ghetto, but he had no choice. He and his wife, Ziuvia Lubetkin, were both active ZOB members and had planned to die together fighting the Nazis. Now Lubetkin replaced her husband as the organization's second in command, while Zuckerman posed as a Polish businessman as he actively pursued the ZOB's interests.

To exit the ghetto, Zuckerman bribed the gate guard, then used the organization's connections to establish new headquarters in a small apartment. It was vital for him to resume contact with the Home Army, since the Polish underground had ceased communications with ZOB agents after Arie Wilner's arrest. Zuckerman had only been on the other side of the wall a short time when he and the other ZOB members working outside the ghetto received a message from Mordechai Anielewicz underscoring the rebels' desperate need for weapons and assistance from outside sources.

Anielewicz was especially concerned about imminent Nazi retaliation. On March 18, along with several other ZOB members, he had ambushed and killed two Baltic soldiers under the SS command who had earned themselves a reputation for robbing and murdering large numbers of Warsaw Jews. A German soldier who intervened was also wounded in the attack. Aware of the Nazis' appetite for vengeance, the ZOB commander in chief feared that they might strike immediately and that the Jews would lack sufficient guns and bullets to defend their people.

Anielewicz's suspicions were not unfounded. Only hours after the incident, Nazi soldiers had entered the area and blocked off a small portion of the central ghetto. One hundred fifty occupants were selected at random and shot on the spot. At that point, the frustrated ghetto rebels felt they would go to any lengths to secure weapons with which to fight back.

The situation's urgency made Zuckerman more keenly aware than ever of his pivotal role. It was essential that he succeed, and finally, on April 12, the Home Army indicated its willingness to resume dialogue with the Jewish organization. Yet Zuckerman came away from their first meeting dissatisfied.

The Polish underground revealed that it wasn't willing to actively assist the ZOB in preparing for a Nazi attack on the ghetto. Its officers stressed that they would only help Jews escape to the forests, where they could fight alongside the Home Army as partisans. These Polish underground representatives added that a member of the ghetto's Judenrat had specifically requested that the ZOB not be given weapons, as the council felt that an armed rebellion would only worsen the Jews' fate.

But ZOB members were convinced that the Warsaw Jews' prospects could not be worsened, since the Nazis planned to kill them all in any case. Yitzhak Zuckerman emphatically insisted that his group's purpose was to defend the ghetto and that its members could not leave to fight in the forest while other Jews remained vulnerable. Following the meeting, Zuckerman had a letter smuggled into the ghetto instructing his wife, Ziuvia, and Mordechai Anielewicz to capture the Judenrat member who had acted to defeat them. He also continued his efforts to make the Polish underground see things the ZOB's way.

Ironically, just a few days later, crates of automatic weapons, rifles, handguns, and grenades were smuggled into the ghetto by a Polish army officer named Captain Henryk Iwanski. But instead of supplying the ZOB with the arms, the captain delivered them to another ghetto rebellion group, known as the Jewish Military Organization, or the ZZW. The ZZW was not affiliated with the ZOB fighters, although both organizations were working toward the same goal.

Even though Captain Iwanski was a Christian Pole, he had been instrumental in establishing the ZZW. While fighting alongside a Jewish Polish-army lieutenant named David Appelbojm during the Nazi invasion, Iwanski had become quite close with the Jewish officer. Appelbojm had told the captain that he feared that the Jews were particularly at risk under Nazi domination. Iwanski had agreed. The captain was among the minority of gentile Poles who felt sympathetically toward the country's Jews. He also firmly believed that any group willing to fight the Germans should be viewed as an ally and supported to the best of the underground's ability.

Appelbojm had begun to form his own ghetto network of trustworthy fighters, and in December 1939 he had signed an agreement making the newly conceived organization a unit of the Home Army. The ZZW quickly expanded and was fortunate to have Captain Iwanski's ardent support. Under his direction, the group amassed additional weapons. It also secured the help of several Polish underground officers in training the new ghetto fighters in the weapons' proper use. Iwanski and his superiors purposely neglected to secure permission for these activities from the Home Army's top command, as they were aware of the existing anti-Semitism and had seen the ZOB's pleas for assistance ignored. So while the ZOB was left to beg for discarded pistols, the ZZW gathered a fair supply of rifles and automatic weaponry.

Ideally, the ZOB and the ZZW should have merged, but the organizations were too ideologically diverse to do so. The ZOB members tended to be prolabor and idealistic. They were against authoritarian military groups and had only resorted to taking up arms as a means of survival.

Many ZZW members, on the other hand, had stressed the importance of discipline and military training even prior to the Nazi invasion. While the ZOB rebels planned to fight to their deaths in the ghetto, the ZZW did not encourage its members to launch suicidal assaults. Instead, once the ghetto battle was clearly lost, they planned to escape with their weapons and fight the Germans in the forests with the Home Army. To ensure their escape from the ghetto, as well as to smuggle in arms and supplies, the ZZW constructed an elaborate network of underground tunnels and bunkers connecting the ghetto to Warsaw's gentile sector.

However, despite their differences, both the ZOB and the ZZW planned—as allies—to fight the upcoming Nazi offensive, and periodically met to determine the best approach to the task. The ZOB had nearly 800 members, which made it about double the size of the ZZW, but ZZW fighters had better military training and superior arms.

As these Jewish underground fighters prepared for battle, the ZOB's influence grew in the ghetto. In time, its authority appeared to surpass that of the Judenrat's, whose members, for the most part, still dutifully carried out the Nazis' decrees. At times the ZOB even made wealthy Judenrat members contribute to the rebels' cause through forceful measures.

In one such instance, they targeted Judenrat chief Marek Lichtenbaum, who was deeply hated in the ghetto for implementing the Nazis' whims at his people's expense. Lichtenbaum had replaced Adam Czerniakow as Judenrat chief after Czerniakow took his own life, in September 1942, when he could no longer tolerate assisting the Germans in deporting Jews to death camps. Czerniakow had tried to leave the Judenrat as early as January 26, 1940. As he indicated in his diary: "I asked the SS to be relieved from the chairmanship since I felt it impossible to manage the community under these conditions. They replied that this would be inadvisable." In a parting letter to the Judenrat, Czerniakow indicated that death was better than a life of cooperation with those determined to murder the Jews. Just prior to taking a potassium cyanide capsule, he wrote: "I am powerless. My heart trembles in sorrow and compassion. I can no longer bear all this. My act will prove to everyone what is the right thing to do."[1]

Lichtenbaum, however, lacked his predecessor's scruples, and continued to do the Germans' bidding. Though he had ample funds, when the ZOB attempted to tax him to support the revolt, he refused to contribute. To make certain he relented, ZOB members kidnapped Lichtenbaum's son and threatened not to return him until they received the desired sum. The Judenrat chief agreed to their terms, and the boy, who'd been well cared for, was promptly returned unharmed. Many in the ghetto viewed the incident as a turning point of sorts. If the ZOB could control the Judenrat, it was clear that the Nazi-established Jewish council was losing its grip on the ghetto.

The ZOB's dramatically enhanced power was especially evident in the ghetto following its effective halt of the January 18, 1943, deportation. The Nazis' retreat inspired a new sense of respect and admiration for the group among some Warsaw Jews who had initially refused to take the rebels seriously. The ZOB members now ardently sought to convince ghetto residents that they were being sent to extermination centers rather than to work camps. For this reason, they were urged not to board the Nazi deportation transports. The rebels spread their message through leaflets and posters placed in strategic areas of the ghetto.

ZOB members even infiltrated German ghetto factories to convince the workers of the importance of fighting back. Arguing that it was better to support the resistance movement than to facilitate the Nazi plans for their people's extermination, the ZOB quickly won loyal converts. Once the German factory owners sensed their laborers' shift in attitude, they ordered Judenrat chief Lichtenbaum to ensure his people's compliance. But while acknowledging the power shift to the ZOB, Lichtenbaum admitted that he was unable to control the workers. For all intents and purposes, the ZOB had assumed charge of the ghetto.

The German entrepreneurs were determined to counter the ZOB's influence, since a decline in worker productivity could result in a considerable financial loss to them. Now they tried to ease the workers' anxiety over possible deportation and to promise incentives to ensure their compliance.

One factory owner established a day-care center for his workers' young children, assuming that his employees would not revolt if they knew that their children would continue to be well cared for. Yet soon afterward, the deceitful entrepreneur secretly cooperated with the SS in arranging for the children to be taken from the nursery and put on trains to extermination centers while their unsuspecting parents were at work. However, at the last minute, word of the atrocity rapidly spread through the plant and the parents rushed from the factory to beg the owner to save their children.

Pretending that the young people's removal was an SS scheme, the seemingly outraged German businessman ordered that the children be returned to the nursery. The parents breathed a sigh of relief, but their children were actually only temporarily safe. Soon afterward, the factory owner called for another truck to come to the nursery, where he personally assisted in swiftly removing the children before their parents could find out. Once again he blamed the cunning trick on the SS and claimed to have been completely unaware of it. These hideous measures only seemed to strengthen the ZOB's resolve and the belief among the remaining ghetto residents that they had to fight back.

In their efforts to eliminate the entire Warsaw ghetto, the

Nazis decided to move the German factories nearer to the extermination centers. The workers were to be moved along with the machinery, to ensure a steady source of slave labor for Germany's wartime needs prior to having these people killed. Once the businesses were safely out of the ghetto, the area could be leveled without negative consequences for the German war effort or gentile business owners.

The ZOB viewed the factory removal and the workers' transfer as a serious blow to both the ghetto's and the Warsaw Jews' continued existence. And when a factory manager tried to evacuate his plant's equipment and furniture, Jewish workers managed to block the move. As a warning to other business owners to leave the factories where they were, ZOB rebels set fire to the facility later that night, destroying much of the building and its contents.

In another instance, trucks carrying factory equipment to the railway were torched by a ZOB unit. The Jewish workers who had followed the vehicles after agreeing to be relocated to the facility's new site had a change of heart and scattered during the episode's commotion. Although most escaped, 60 workers were captured by the German soldiers guarding the trucks. Fortunately, all were freed in a later ZOB raid on the building where they were being held.

By then, some of the German industrialists who had successfully operated in the ghetto began to panic. They realized that many of the Jewish workers who had made them rich in the hope of being spared had undergone a change. Now their laborers refused to believe any more Nazi propaganda and were prepared to fight.

The minority of Jews who'd thrown their lot in with the Nazis soon found that they had much to fear as well. One such individual was Leon Skosowski, a formerly wealthy young Jew who was determined to do whatever was necessary to survive. Skosowski was extremely helpful to the Germans in sending countless ghetto Jews to their deaths. In return for his fruitful cooperation, he was afforded an abundance of food and liquor, along with admission to ghetto nightclubs and Nazi-sponsored brothels. Gestapo agents even rotated his car on a weekly basis to make it more difficult for Jewish rebels to locate and punish him for collaborating with the enemy.

Nevertheless, an armed band of ZZW fighters managed to burst in on one of the wild parties Skosowski was known for. They ordered everyone except the host and four other Nazi informers to leave immediately. Skosowski begged the rebels to allow them to purchase their freedom, but the resistance fighters would not be bribed. Instead they sent forth a shower of bullets, killing the four traitorous guests. Though badly wounded, Leon Skosowski managed to escape. Nevertheless, the rebel forces had undeniably become a power to be reckoned with. Jews who deliberately betrayed their own people could no longer do so safely.

The ghetto's final destruction was initially to be orchestrated by the SS and Warsaw's police commander, Colonel Ferdinand von Sammern-Frankenegg. However, SS chief Heinrich Himmler had begun to doubt that the low-ranking officer could adequately accomplish the feat. The Nazis regarded the remaining ghetto Jews as the cleverest and most resourceful of any they'd encountered in Warsaw. These individuals had survived hunger, disease, and abject poverty. Even in the face of unspeakable brutality and extreme deprivation, they had managed to organize to fight their oppressors.

Himmler had been briefed on the ghetto fighters' valiant response to the Nazis' attempted January action and knew that since then the Jewish underground had become even better organized and equipped. Therefore, to ensure the operation's swift success, Himmler had SS major general Jürgen Stroop dispatched to Warsaw.

General Stroop was thought to be especially well suited for the task of wiping out Warsaw's Jews. The slaughters already credited to him included destroying a Czechoslovakian partisan movement, killing over 2,000 Poles in another part of the country, and the bloody massacre of a sizable band of Soviet partisans.

Blond, blue-eyed Jürgen Stroop took tremendous pride in his typically Aryan appearance, and rarely passed a mirror or a window without stopping to gaze at his reflection. Checking to ensure that he embodied an idealized Nazi image, Stroop made certain that his boots were always highly polished and that he carried his whip with an air of defiant arrogance.

Stroop's voracious appetite for snuffing out opposition to the Nazi regime was highly valued by his superiors. He had been picked to be part of a special group of promising young SS officers who studied repression and terrorist tactics in a course taught by Himmler himself. From there he had rapidly risen through the ranks of the SS.

Jürgen Stroop had also been an ideal candidate for the strict discipline and unquestioning loyalty required of SS officers. His father was a policeman who had ruled his household with a firm hand. In fact, both Stroop's parents regularly subjected him and his siblings to severe and prolonged beatings for even minor signs of disobedience.

As a child, Stroop had developed a strong sense of Germanic pride. His father often spoke to him of the "fatherland" with genuine patriotic zeal. The boy especially loved holiday military parades, with their uniformed marching soldiers, prancing horses, and nationalistic band music.

**Nazi general Stroop with his soldiers
inside the ghetto**

Stroop would much rather have been around armed soldiers than sitting in a classroom. He had never been very much of a student and at first had decided not to continue his education after elementary school. However, realizing that his lack of education might be detrimental to his career aspirations, Stroop later resumed his studies and earned a high-school diploma at the age of twenty-seven.

Prior to Hitler's rise to power, Stroop hadn't felt any particular animosity toward local Jews—he'd even found himself attracted to more than one beautiful Jewish girl. But after his indoctrination to Nazi racial theories, Stroop turned against the Jewish population with a bitter vehemence.

There was little doubt in the SS high command that Stroop would destroy the Warsaw ghetto. It would be a special type of confrontation, designed and executed by a special type of general. This was not to be a battle waged for territory or to gain a political advantage, but rather to eliminate a group of people the Nazis regarded as inferior. Stroop had no intention of taking prisoners—he planned to murder all the Jews left in the ghetto, in the hope of creating a "racially pure" German empire.

Southern Sr. High Media Center
Harwood, Maryland 20776

CHAPTER 4

The Beginning
of the End

T he Nazis had scheduled the destruction of the Warsaw ghetto for April 19, 1943. The demise of the area and the Jews living in it was to be a gift for Hitler's birthday on the following day. April 19 was a special day for the Jews as well, but for a very different reason. It marked the beginning of the Passover holiday, which celebrates the freeing of the Jews from bondage in ancient Egypt.

Despite their present oppression, many of the Warsaw ghetto Jews planned to hold Passover seders (special ceremonial meals) while hidden from the Nazis in their underground bunkers. During the previous week, the ghetto had bustled with activity in preparation for the holiday. The bunkers were scrubbed clean, and bottles of wine that had been stored away for this special occasion suddenly appeared in the makeshift kitchen areas. Most families that could afford to had saved for weeks to be able to enjoy a decent holiday meal. Many who had lost their families were invited to celebrate with friends and neighbors in nearby bunkers.

But just days before the holiday, the Jewish resistance organizations noted an ominous incident that filled them with dread. First Lieutenant Karl Brandt, chief of the Warsaw Gestapo's Jewish division, came to the ghetto to visit with Judenrat members. Pretending to be upset about the fate of Jewish children, the Nazi officer stated that the young people must be given fresh vegetables. He also suggested that a playground be constructed for them. On the surface, the lieutenant's visit seemed innocent enough, perhaps even amicable. But by now, the Jewish fighters were all too familiar with Nazi treachery and reasoned that Brandt's visit signaled an imminent attack.

About 48 hours later, the day before Passover (April 18), their worst fears were confirmed. Mordechai Anielewicz first received word of the expected Nazi onslaught from a Jewish ghetto police officer who was actually a ZOB spy. The ghetto fighters were soon bombarded with tidbits from their key sources concerning the Nazis' intentions. By two o'clock that afternoon, SS troops in Warsaw had begun to mobilize for battle. Within the next four hours, the ghetto was completely surrounded by a sea of well-armed Nazis determined to destroy it once and for all. They planned to attack early on the morning of Passover, hoping to catch the Jews off guard as they prepared for the evening holiday service and meal.

Realizing that what they had both feared and anticipated was about to occur, resistance workers speedily told the ghetto residents to prepare for the German attack. People quickly gathered up their last-minute supplies and headed for the relative safety of their underground bunkers. A number of Jewish resistance fighters put on the Nazi uniforms they had previously pilfered from Ghetto factories. By dressing this way, they hoped both to shift battle positions with greater ease and to create some degree of confusion within the German ranks.

Although the fighters had wished for a last-minute shipment of weapons from the Home Army, they had received only what some in the ghetto construed as shallow sympathy. Nevertheless, the Jewish resistance fighters were determined to devise the best battle strategy possible with whatever resources were available to them. Various ZOB lookouts assumed key positions within the ghetto, from which they could spot any enemy movements. The minute Nazi troops entered, one of these rebels was to throw out a grenade to alert the others immediately.

The Jewish rebels checked and rechecked their weapons and ammunition. Blankets filled with Molotov cocktails were delivered to the various bands of fighters throughout the ghetto. They placed sandbags in the windows to absorb Nazi bullets and left overturned wagons and cupboards at strategic points to block the enemy's access to vital passageways.

As the hours passed, further confirmation of the Germans' intentions reached rebel leaders. Late in the afternoon on April 18, Gestapo agents told the Judenrat that Nazi troops would attack the ghetto early the next morning. Then they locked the men in the building and left them to face the assault with the other residents.

However, one Judenrat member escaped and immediately related what he'd learned to a ZZW commander. The ZZW leader in turn relayed the message to ZOB leader Mordechai Anielewicz. Ironically, the men had planned to meet that very night to work out ways of better blending ZZW and ZOB forces. But there was no longer time for that. The 22 ZOB groups and 3 ZZW units would have to fight for the same cause in different parts of the ghetto. Instead of enjoying a holiday seder commemorating their ancestors' liberation, the Warsaw Jews would spend Passover battling for the lives of their people.

On the gentile side of Warsaw, General Stroop prepared for the upcoming confrontation in a more relaxed manner. He'd previously inspected the ghetto, studied the situation, and was fully prepared to take over if the lower-ranking Colonel von Sammern-Frankenegg failed to crush the Jewish rebellion immediately.

That night, as the Jewish rebels contemplated ways to stretch their meager rations and supplies through what could prove to be a lengthy struggle, Stroop dined alone in his tasteful yet luxurious room. He wore an expensive pair of silk pajamas, a smoking jacket, and a rare, imported cologne. He had decided to order his favorite foods for dinner, which included dumplings, roast beef and potatoes, and a bottle of fine wine. After dining, he relaxed in a comfortable chair while enjoying an imported cigar. Stroop telephoned an aide to give him an early wake-up call, and shortly thereafter went to sleep in a bed complete with feather pillows and scented sheets.

The day of the Nazis' attack was warm and springlike. It was April 19, 1943. Birds sang in the trees and flowers had begun to bloom. Bloodshed and killing seemed particularly out of place on such a day, but that was precisely the Nazis' intention as nearly 900 men marched toward the ghetto, gaily singing. In addition to the German soldiers, there were also Ukrainians, now serving under the SS command, whose virulent anti-Semitism made them ideal for this assignment.

The well-armed group was there to crush any sign of Jewish resistance, and to ensure its success, the troops were accompanied by both a tank and two armored cars. Besides the men entering the ghetto, the Nazis had summoned an ample backup force to Warsaw. A reinforcement squad of 2,000 men stood ready to assist in the ghetto's demolition, while another 7,000 were on hand in case the anticipated revolt spread to the rest of Warsaw. Despite their past loyalty to the Nazis, a swarm of Jewish police officers were placed at the troops' front to shield the Aryans from rebel bullets. Those who refused to cooperate or attempted to run away were shot on the spot.

Colonel von Sammern-Frankenegg was especially anxious for the speedy destruction of the Jewish ghetto, with a minimum of German casualties. He was aware of the fact that Himmler had sent General Stroop to Warsaw to intercede if the operation failed and knew that his career hung in the balance. Von Sammern-Frankenegg's strategy seemed uncomplicated and direct. Since the ghetto had been divided into three districts, he planned to strike one section at a time, beginning with the central ghetto. The colonel felt confident of his men and his plan—he was sure he would succeed and would not be turned back as he had been in January.

Meanwhile, within the ghetto, Jewish resistance fighters saw to last-minute details as they readied themselves for battle. Mordechai Anielewicz visited the various strategically fortified posts, reminding his soldiers that bullets were in short supply and should only be used to pierce Nazi flesh. About half an hour later, the first rebel lookout spied the oncoming troops. Because only the sea of Jewish police heading the invading column could initially be seen, the resistance fighters held their fire until the Nazis were in full view. At that point, the first grenade was thrown out, signaling the rebels to attack.

The grenade exploded in the midst of enemy troops and was swiftly followed by a heavy downpour of rebel grenades, homemade bombs, and bullets. One German soldier who had caught fire after being hit with a Molotov cocktail ran screaming down the street, filling the others with fear. The enemy soldiers had anticipated some rebel resistance, but thought that there would be only a minimal number of half-starved fighters, armed with just clenched fists and a few pistols and lead pipes.

Caught in an unexpected display of firepower, the stunned troops panicked. They ran in all directions, some yelling, "The Jews are armed!" The enemy soldiers tried to hide in the vacant ghetto stores, hallways, and behind walls and gates. In instances where there wasn't ample hiding space, German soldiers pushed the Ukrainians back out into the street.

However, the rebel fighters concentrated on foiling the enemy's escape, rapidly opening fire wherever the invading troops sought cover. The Aryan soldiers remained easy targets, since the Jews could monitor their movements without exposing themselves. In one instance, a young Jewish woman shot at a huddle of soldiers from a window across the street from where they were trying to hide. Although she quickly ducked to avoid their return fire, one of the soldiers caught a glimpse of the shooter and cried out, "My God, a woman is firing." Hearing his outburst, the woman chuckled to herself as she saw a member of the supposed Aryan master race trembling at the sight of his opponent.

Attempting to regroup after the shock of the Jewish assault, the Nazi soldiers slowly began to leave their hiding places. They mercilessly lashed the Ukrainian soldiers with their riding crops to force them to resume their battle positions. Meanwhile, the Jewish attack persisted. The Aryan forces tried to fight the hidden snipers and grenade throwers for nearly another half hour before fleeing the ghetto battlefront.

Their retreat was short-lived. Before long, the Nazis reappeared. This time, however, the soldiers' procession was led by Colonel von Sammern-Frankenegg's tank and two armored cars. The Jewish rebels carefully tracked the vehicles' route, and when the tank reached a building where a rebel battalion was stationed, the fighters unleashed a storm of grenades and Molotov cocktails on it. The tank caught fire and its crew burned alive. After one of the Nazis' two armored cars burst into flames, the other vehicle rapidly retreated.

As many Nazi soldiers quickly left the fray, most of the German dead and wounded remained where they had fallen. But when Nazi ambulances arrived to remove them, the freedom fighters interrupted their rescue and retrieval efforts with a barrage of bullets. They felt no sympathy for those who had brutally murdered their parents, children, and friends.

Following their temporary victory, the Jewish rebels excitedly hugged one another and exchanged triumphant stories of downing Germans. They listened attentively to the BBC and Polish underground accounts of the morning's miraculous events. As the rebel leaders formulated further battle plans, other fighters took care of immediate practical concerns. They gathered whatever weapons had been abandoned by the Germans and removed the dead Nazi soldiers' uniforms and helmets. With the present shortage of supplies, nothing could be left to chance or wasted.

Only one Jew was wounded during the fighting. He had

been so determined to avenge his people that he gave too little thought to his own safety. Instead of shooting at the Germans from behind a protective barrier, he had fired his weapon while leaning over a balcony. This enabled him to aim more accurately, but it also left the young fighter fully exposed to enemy fire. Each time he hit a German target he would kick up his foot as a sign to those within the apartment to cheer. But soon after he downed a group of Germans, the young man's leg remained still. Realizing that he had been hit, the cheering stopped as the others quickly brought their friend inside.

While the rebel fighters rejoiced in their early-morning victory, they were certain that the Germans would soon launch a second assault. In fact, General Stroop had been preparing for the attack since receiving the humiliating reports of how well-trained German soldiers ran for their lives from a small band of ill-equipped, haphazardly trained Jewish rebels.

Word of the early-morning retreat had quickly reached the Nazi high command as well, and Himmler personally telephoned Stroop, instructing him to relieve von Sammern-Frankenegg of his post and assume charge of the operation. Fearing that the ghetto revolt might spread to other areas of Nazi-occupied Poland, Himmler insisted that all German forces in Poland be put on alert. Although he believed the Home Army was capable of little more than limited sabotage and sniper attacks, he hoped to quell the rebellion quickly and counted on Polish anti-Semitism to limit the gentile Poles' identification with the Jews under fire.

Stroop immediately devised a new battle plan to take the ghetto. While von Sammern-Frankenegg had attempted to capture the central ghetto in a single assault, Stroop decided to send in small units of soldiers to attack and destroy the rebel strongholds one at a time. He hoped that once the rebel core had been defeated, the other ghetto residents would realize that further resistance was pointless.

The SS general also provided his men with a significantly better backup force than von Sammern-Frankenegg had. Stroop used twice as many officers and 50 percent more soldiers to attack the ghetto. Weapons and artillery for the confrontation were comparably reinforced. The Nazi soldiers would now be supported by additional tanks, armored cars, antiaircraft guns, and a howitzer.

The ghetto fighters also tried to prepare for the second round of their fight with the Nazis, but they had far fewer resources at their disposal. Some of the young men and women who were still exhausted from the first fray had even fallen asleep clutching their weapons. Their respite from battle was short. Before long, a messenger arrived at the ZOB command station to announce that the Germans were again in the ghetto. The Jews had just seconds to assume their battle positions; moments later, gunfire could be heard coming from outside the building.

German soldiers in front of a nearby warehouse were shooting at rebel targets from behind a protective barrier of mattresses. However, fearing rebel fire, the soldiers barely raised their heads to aim, and consistently missed their marks. The Jews, with far more at stake, took greater risks, and while they fired fewer shots, to conserve ammunition, they tended to hit their targets.

The rebels' most decisive gain came when a Molotov cocktail struck the Nazis' mattress barricade and set it on fire. The Germans quickly ran for cover, but the Jews made certain that they didn't get very far. Stroop's tanks and heavy artillery proved to be of little assistance to his forces in this confrontation. They remained behind the troops to avoid being hit by a ghetto-made bomb, but at that distance, the weaponry did not take a significant toll.

It looked as though there might be a repeat of the rebels' early-morning victory when the tide of battle began to turn. The Germans had started throwing their own incendiary bombs, and one of them hit a rebel station and caused an explosion and fire. Weeks earlier, the rebels had designed an escape route for themselves in the event that they had to flee quickly from the premises undetected. They would go to a nearby building, which they would reach through a series of interconnecting attic passageways they had created by hacking out portions of the floors and walls in critically situated buildings.

However, the small rebel group hadn't proceeded very far through the attic maze when another Jewish fighter coming from the opposite direction warned them that the Nazis had captured the building toward which they were heading. At that point, the fighters saw few available alternatives. They couldn't go on, and the building they had just left was now in flames. They could only wait in the attic passage while two members of the group left to scout for other attic openings.

But a few minutes later, smoke from the burning building they had left began to filter into the dark attic space the rebels now occupied. Before long, the young fighters' eyes teared as they choked on the smoke that flooded the attic. The fire was spreading, and beams of smoldering wood began to fall close by. The rebels felt the floor beneath them start to weaken as well.

To make matters worse, a group of Nazi soldiers had discovered the rebels' attic passageways and were now approaching the trapped fighters from the adjoining attic. But when the enemy came closer, the Jews fired their weapons and hit one of the Germans. Unable to clearly see the rebels through the smoke, and surprised by the sudden shots, the other Nazis quickly retreated. Although the rebels were momentarily safe from the Germans, they were soon nearly overcome by the dense cloud of smoke that now blanketed the attic. The sickened fighters stumbled about the small space, gasping for air. Some lay on the floor, struggling to breathe and thinking that the end was near.

Fortunately, the scouts returned moments later, having found another path to pursue among the interconnecting attics. The new route was exceptionally narrow and the weakened fighters had to cling to one another as they made their way through the slender passages, but they eventually emerged into an outside courtyard. They soon came upon an underground bunker where a number of Jews were hiding, and hoped they could remain there until they were able to resume fighting.

But even though the rebels risked their lives to defend these people, they soon learned that they weren't welcome. The bunker inhabitants felt that things would be worse for them if the Germans were to find them with the armed rebels. After a number of people fled from the hiding place, the fighters voluntarily left in order not to jeopardize the others. Without giving themselves time to rest, they made their way through the interconnecting attics in search of another battle station from which to fight.

Throughout the battle, General Stroop continued to send fresh German troops into the ghetto, and while they were unable to capture a single rebel fighter, hundreds of Jews who didn't have bunkers were taken prisoner. The Nazis brought them to a large courtyard that already contained piles of lifeless Jewish bodies lying on the blood-soaked soil. These were prisoners shot by German soldiers within the past hour to avoid overcrowding at the deportation plaza, where other prisoners were being loaded onto trains leaving for extermination camps.

Stroop was instrumental in deciding who would live and die. He chose his victims on whims, and that afternoon Stroop ordered all the redheads shot, along with the individuals whom he found least attractive. The body count became so massive that at one point the German soldiers had to stop shooting and stack the corpses to make room for the incoming prisoners. This brutal procedure continued through the afternoon, with the Nazis only occasionally pausing to allow their weapons to cool off.

Even as the fighting and civilian executions continued, a number of escape and rescue attempts were tried. The small contingent of Home Army officers willing to support the revolt used the surrounding chaos to spirit Jews out of the ghetto. Dressed as firemen, two such Christian Poles approached a German SS officer to ask permission to put out a fire in the Church of the Virgin Mary—the only Christian place of worship situated behind the ghetto wall. Realizing that the officer they'd approach was already intoxicated, they offered him cash with which to purchase still more liquor, and moments later they were permitted to drive their fire truck into the ghetto.

In under an hour, more than 50 Jews were carried to safety. With several additional trips into the ghetto, supposedly to extinguish the flames, still more ghetto residents left, hidden beneath the fire-fighting equipment. The scheme might have continued throughout the afternoon had not

Jews in the Warsaw ghetto are rounded up and searched before being executed.

another German officer become suspicious of the fire-fighting efforts and stopped the truck to inspect it. Although he discovered the illicit human cargo, both the Jews and their Christian rescuers were saved when the quick-thinking driver offered the German his gold watch and three bottles of vodka in exchange for their freedom.

Some civilian Jews hoping to flee the ghetto while the fighting continued resorted to desperate measures to escape. One father risked being shot on sight by German soldiers as he approached the guardhouse to offer the guards a substantial cash sum to allow his family to leave the ghetto. To his amazement, they agreed, so he tried to save some of his friends and neighbors by inquiring whether other families could come along if they brought enough cash with them. The guards agreed, provided that they leave in groups of no more than five and that everyone was out before the next guard shift came on duty.

When the father returned to his building with the news, those who could afford the bribe immediately prepared to leave. They agreed that women and children should go first, but when the sizable group reached a gate, a young man cried out, "We all leave together, or no one goes." Panic broke out as dozens of people hurriedly pushed forward toward the exit. Fearing that their superiors would notice the rush of people, the gate guards began firing into the crowd. Some fell dead, while the rest scattered to look for last-minute hiding places. The young man who spoke out had inadvertently made certain that no one left.

In the meantime, the rebel fighters and German soldiers had turned the ghetto into a war zone. Unlike his inept predecessor, General Stroop was determined to move his troops into the heart of the central ghetto and extend their reach into the productive ghetto soon afterward. But their forward advance was not as easy as Stroop had envisioned because now the Nazis had to contend with ZZW fighters.

This rebel force was more firmly entrenched in its territory than the ZOB rebels the Nazis had fought earlier in the day. The ZZW also had superior weaponry, and its battle plan entailed confusing and disabling the Germans by continually shifting its forces between various strategic battle stations.

ZZW headquarters were situated in the ghetto's most heavily fortified building. Beneath the structure was a tunnel leading to Warsaw's gentile district, while on the roof, rebels crouched between the ghetto's only two heavy machine guns, waiting for the enemy. As Stroop's men approached the ZZW's terrain, they found themselves engulfed in a ring of enemy fire. In response, the Nazis fired into the surrounding ghetto storefronts, where they believed the ZZW fighters were hiding. But their bullets merely struck empty buildings, as the rebels had immediately taken cover in new locations.

The Germans' plight worsened when rebels stationed at the machine guns fired at the Nazi troops below, downing significant numbers. Amazed that the Jews had machine guns, Stroop's tank drivers hurriedly backed their machines off to avoid being hit, leaving the bulk of the Nazi soldiers at the rebels' mercy.

ZZW fighters savored the sweet taste of victory as the Nazi casualties continued to mount. To further humiliate the Germans, they hoisted both the Zionist and Polish flags alongside the machine guns. The Zionist flag represented the political movement to establish a national Jewish homeland in Palestine. As the flags were raised sufficiently high to be seen on the gentile side of the wall, the Nazis feared that these proudly waving symbols of freedom might incite the Christian Poles to revolt as well.

While the fighting continued, a number of German industrialists whose factories were now in jeopardy arrived to survey the battle scene. While witnessing their Jewish workers furiously fighting, they thought that Stroop's harsh military response might result in the destruction of their labor force, supplies, and equipment.

A few of the businessmen convinced General Stroop to temporarily halt his troops' fire, to allow them to make a personal plea to the workers to report for deportation. At this point, they still hoped that their supplies and equipment could be relocated to labor camps staffed by the young, healthy Jews the SS intended to work to death. Although the workers knew that the vast majority of those who surrendered would either be immediately shot or sent to extermination centers, the Germans used a loudspeaker to assure the ghetto residents that those who gave themselves up would be spared and put to work in pleasant environments. As in the past, the Germans tried to convince ghetto residents that the rebel fighters' irresponsible actions would lead to the demise of all of Warsaw's Jews.

Hours later, one of the leading ghetto industrialists received a telephone call at his factory headquarters from a man claiming to be one of his workers. The German entrepreneur was told that a large group of Jews had decided to volunteer for relocation after all. The businessman enthusiastically responded to the caller's request for an early-morning escort to lead the workers out of the productive ghetto the following day. After hanging up the telephone receiver, the Nazi businessman still had no idea that the man he'd spoken to was actually a ZZW agent planning an ambush.

General Stroop had his troops prepare to leave the ghetto

at about four o'clock in the afternoon to avoid fighting the rebels in the dark. Although a significant number of Germans had died that day, the troops marched out singing an anti-Semitic song to lift their spirits. The exhausted German soldiers looked relieved, believing that they'd survived the first day of fighting.

But the fighting wasn't over for the rebels, who had planted a bomb near where the troops were about to exit. As soon as the passing soldiers triggered the bomb, ZOB fighters planned to jump out from their hiding places and shoot those Nazis who survived the explosion.

But even though ZOB fighters had checked the bomb daily to ensure that it was in working order, that afternoon the device failed to go off. Refusing to abandon a valuable opportunity to catch the enemy off guard, the Jews threw a slew of grenades and Molotov cocktails at the exiting Nazis. There were massive German casualties, and those soldiers left standing barely made it to safety in Warsaw's gentile district.

After dark, ghetto residents began to emerge from their underground bunkers and other hiding places. They were afraid to remain outside too long, but were anxious to have a breath of fresh air and to learn the fate of friends and loved ones who had fought the Germans.

The Jews had valiantly fought back that day. Yet their lack of manpower, ammunition, and money was a continual reminder of the odds they faced and of what lay ahead.

A building bursts into flames as
the Nazis invade the ghetto.

CHAPTER 5

The Onslaught

Stroop rose early on the second day of the ghetto assault. Although he appeared optimistic and confident to the troops, he was troubled about his men's incentive and morale. He wondered if the Jews would present as united and difficult a front as they had the previous day. After observing his men run for cover at the sound of rebel fire, Stroop also questioned if they had the courage to engage in combat with enemy soldiers who knew that they would be killed if captured.

The general had altered his battle plan for the day's attack. He would split the men at his disposal into units of 36 soldiers. They were to be scattered throughout the ghetto in an attempt to regain the territory they had invaded the previous day, but were forced to abandon before dark.

Hoping to break the resistance movement's spine, the Nazis tried to intimidate their enemy as they entered the ghetto that morning. From behind their fortified posts, Jewish fighters observed a flow of German forces that made the previous day's invasion look like a trickle. Now seemingly endless columns of foot soldiers, led by Nazi motorcyclists and followed by armored cars, poured into the ghetto streets.

However, determined not to fall victim to the oncoming Germans, the rebels attacked moments after the Nazis set foot in the ghetto. The roads filled with smoke and the odor of gunpowder as the early-morning invaders were greeted with a shower of grenades and a simultaneous spray of bullets. Fully expecting to strike first, a large portion of the stunned Nazi soldiers acted to save themselves rather than to immediately retaliate. Some of the Nazis near the ghetto's entrance simply ran from its confines, lying flat on their stomachs on the gentile side of the wall to avoid any stray enemy bullets that might come from the other side. Many of those Germans deeper in the ghetto ran into empty shops, factories, and apartment buildings for cover. Nearly a third of the Nazi soldiers who'd approached the area were now either dead or wounded.

Once the Germans regained their composure, small clusters of soldiers began turning their machine guns on the rows of ghetto buildings, hoping to hit any unseen assailants lurking within. However, in their zeal the Nazis neglected to omit the factories in which German businessmen had remained, hoping to protect their raw materials and machinery. After one of the ghetto's most influential Aryan businessmen was hit in the hand, his chief assistant came running out of the building, wildly waving a white handkerchief in each hand and screaming, "Don't shoot, don't shoot! Only Germans are in the shop." In a similar incident, a German industrialist fired his own pistol out a window and loudly urged the soldiers to shoot the enemy rather than their countrymen.

Once the fighting had subsided somewhat, the surviving

German soldiers tried to bring their wounded to the central ghetto, where they hoped they'd be out of the range of fire. However, upon arriving, the soldiers realized that they hadn't reached a safe zone after all. Rebel fighters had followed them through a hidden attic maze, and just as they were about to rest their wounded on the ground, they were hit with a surprise rebel onslaught. The Germans fired back, engaging in a battle that lasted about fifteen minutes. When it was over, nearly a dozen more Nazis had fallen.

In other parts of the ghetto, however, the Germans were more successful. Nazi soldiers, flanked by a tank and flamethrower, had rapidly advanced toward ZZW headquarters. They were anxious to remove the Zionist and Polish flags raised by the rebels the previous day. In response, ZZW fighters relied heavily on rifle fire and Molotov cocktails to fend off the enemy. Although the Jewish fighters disabled a tank, German troop power was more substantial than it had been the day before, and the Nazis kept on coming.

However, the sought-after flags were still protected by rooftop machine gunners and other ZZW rebels stationed with them. The Germans used a flamethrower to torch the roof, but the rebels dodged the flames as they fired on the Nazis below. Before long, the fire burned itself out, and the enemy had still not been able either to capture the building or to remove the flags.

Although the Jews generally fought more bravely than their Nazi counterparts, Stroop's men seized territory in various ghetto areas on the sheer strength of their numbers. Despite their high casualty rate, the German soldiers finally began to feel that they had made some important strides in the battle. And as they optimistically shifted positions, the Nazis never imagined that they were headed directly for the largest bomb the rebels had been able to manufacture.

Less than a block away, a rebel hidden from view sat tightly clutching the detonator switch as he patiently awaited the approach of a sizable number of enemy soldiers. When he saw over 300 Nazis reach the courtyard where the bomb was buried, he pushed the button. For a moment, it felt as though an earthquake had struck. A grotesque mixture of body parts, bricks, glass, and sidewalk flew through the air in the explosion's wake. When it was over, nearly 100 Germans lay dead or wounded where they had landed on the ground.

As General Stroop watched the explosion from a distance, he felt both humiliation and rage. He had sent in more troops than anyone would have thought necessary and armed them with the most technologically advanced weapons. But instead of quelling the Jewish rebellion within hours, many of his men had once more run shrieking from a motley enemy force. Stroop was so incensed by his men's poor performance that when the bomb survivors finally reached safety, he immediately ordered them to go back and not return without the dead and wounded soldiers.

Meanwhile, rebels in the brushmakers' district launched a series of sniper attacks at enemy targets. During the early afternoon, a car carrying three German officers followed by several rows of Nazi soldiers entered the area. Although the Germans didn't know it, their progress through the district was being monitored by rebel lookouts. When the officers' vehicle reached the designated area, one of the Jewish fighters threw a grenade at it from a fourth-floor window. Other rebels posted in buildings on both sides of the street did the same, and within seconds, chaos broke out in the German ranks below.

Pelted with rebel grenades from every direction, the Germans once again panicked. They didn't know where to run for cover, since fleeing to any of the surrounding buildings might result in an enemy confrontation. But it was difficult to think clearly, in any case, as they were soon surrounded by screaming soldiers who'd caught fire during the grenade shower. Adding to the Nazis' distress, a Jewish sharpshooter stationed on a rooftop killed many of those who frantically sought shelter. In the end, only two German soldiers survived the skirmish, and the rebels felt certain that Nazi morale had sunk to a new low.

After hearing what had transpired, General Stroop sought his revenge on the brushmakers' district within the hour. To salvage his pride, he sent in a massive number of troops equipped with antiaircraft guns, flamethrowers, and automatic weapons. The rebels knew that they couldn't possibly take on this incredibly powerful force and realized that they would have to flee. As German soldiers now occupied the buildings they had hoped to escape to, it was clear that one of the rebels would have to leave the group to find a place for them. A young Aryan-looking Jew immediately volunteered for the assignment. He wore a German soldier's uniform, stolen from a ghetto factory months before, and therefore could readily move about among enemy troops. Outside of being detected by the Nazis, the only danger was that of being hit by a Jewish sniper's bullet.

Knowing where many of the bunkers were concealed, the Jew entered one nearby to inquire if the fighting group could take temporary refuge there. Unfortunately, his sudden appearance terrified some of the occupants, who saw his uniform and thought he was a Nazi about to kill them. After calming those within and surveying the dugout, the rebel fighter left anyway. The bunker was already overcrowded and could never have accommodated the number of people he had in mind. The youthful fighter had also sensed that the inhabitants would not want to risk harboring armed rebels. Fortunately, the next bunker he came across had ample space, and its occupants assured him that they would be honored to assist the ghetto defenders.

Most of the rebels in the brushmakers' district made it to safety. Others insisted on remaining at their firing stations too long. Among these was a fighter in his middle forties who the ZOB leadership had initially thought was too old to fight. However, the man insisted on participating, arguing that he was an excellent shot and that he had little left to live for since the Nazis had murdered his family.

Once the others left, only the middle-aged fighter and a small group of his followers stayed on. They shot at the Nazis from the windows on the upper floors of a building, and when the Germans fired back, they rapidly shifted positions. As the enemy soldiers continued to fall, the older fighter yelled out that they'd finally given the Nazis a taste of their own medicine.

Even after a German flamethrower set fire to the building, the middle-aged fighter was among those who refused to leave before inflicting further German casualties. Sadly, the members of the tiny band paid for their heroic feat with their lives. Once the fire became too widespread to escape, they were forced to throw themselves out the windows to avoid being burned alive. Unfortunately, the Nazis waiting below shot them either as they fell through the air or once they hit the pavement.

Miles away, Nazi governor-general Hans Frank, who oversaw various aspects of Germany's domination of Poland, had grown concerned over the Warsaw ghetto rebellion. The

Nazis hadn't counted on any significant Jewish resistance, despite their continued atrocities, but now the Warsaw Jews had become a thorn in their side. Frank was particularly enraged when Hitler empowered Himmler to order a hard and fast put-down of the rebellion, since Frank had long advocated moderation in handling Warsaw's Jewish question. It wasn't that Frank was less than anti-Semitic, but the governor-general feared that if the Jews ardently fought to overthrow Nazi oppression, gentile Poles might refuse to be further subjugated as well. Since Warsaw was a vital transfer station for the German war effort, the Nazis could not afford to have the entire city embroiled in an ongoing battle.

Seeking to safeguard his own reputation and political future, Frank dispatched a letter to one of Hitler's top aides, describing the Warsaw insurrection as potentially dangerous. The letter stressed that since Himmler had been instrumental in determining the soldiers' mode of operation, Frank could not be responsible for any negative consequences. Aware that Stroop had downplayed his troops' inability to capture rebel leaders, Governor-General Frank noted the high number of German casualties and underscored how Nazi troops had already had to use machine guns.

By the close of the rebellion's second day, General Stroop had also become increasingly annoyed by the rebels' fortitude. He called a short meeting of his officers and the ghetto's Aryan industrialists, during which he expressed his frustration at not having ended the rebellion in time for their führer's birthday. Stroop was also disappointed that his men had not rounded up any more civilians than they had the day before.

Due to these setbacks, the general announced a major tactical change in dealing with the rebels. He informed the German businessmen that he could no longer afford to limit ghetto destruction in order to safeguard their property. Although Stroop hesitated to admit it, his reports to Himmler had exaggerated his success in the ghetto. In only two days of fighting, hundreds of Nazi soldiers had been either killed or wounded, but Stroop told Himmler that they had only suffered nine casualties.

General Stroop noted that whatever limited success he'd achieved in the ghetto resulted from having set fire to a number of buildings. Only then did the Jews abandon their hidden bunkers and attic mazes to escape the flames. The embarrassed SS general was determined to put down the surprisingly resilient rebellion, even if he had to burn down the entire ghetto to do it.

Meanwhile, a number of ghetto factory workers decided to leave their hiding places and report for deportation, since German industrialists had previously made their way through the ghetto shouting that this was their last opportunity to do so. The workers could either continue working at the factories' new locations or perish with the ghetto freedom fighters.

Although the industrialists had made similar appeals at the start of battle, no one had accepted their offers. But by now, many of the civilians were forced to face reality. They knew that in the long run the rebels could never defeat the Nazis and thought that this might be their only chance for survival. Of course, they were aware that there were no guarantees in dealing with the Nazis. They had been deceived before and knew that they could be shot before ever boarding a transport or simply shipped off to an extermination camp.

As the Jewish workers contemplated volunteering for deportation, the rebels were devising a scheme to save them from what they were certain would be a fatal choice. The fighters had two possible rescue attempts in mind: They could pretend to be workers and open fire on the enemy when they reached the depot, or they could remain at their posts and shoot the Nazis escorting the truckloads of Jewish laborers to the railway.

The Nazis had given the Jews until noon to report, and while they had expected thousands of people to appear, only several hundred arrived. Many of these individuals were either too frightened, discouraged, or tired to resist any longer—they had decided to leave their fate to chance.

Determining that it would be suicidal to attack the Nazis while among the workers, at noon armed ZOB rebels crouched behind the windows of an abandoned building, hoping to down the Germans escorting the Jews to the railway. While they'd initially intended to kill the vehicles' drivers, the fighters felt that Jews riding in the trucks might too easily be hurt or killed in the process. As an alternative, the resistance fighters only shot at the Nazis walking behind the truck caravan as they searched nearby buildings for Jews in hiding and rounded up stragglers. Although the shooters killed a number of German soldiers, they were disappointed at not having saved many Jews in the process.

Another rebel unit inflicted further damage on the enemy later in the day, attacking a string of trucks carrying Nazi soldiers out of the central ghetto. The Jews threw grenades and Molotov cocktails at the vehicles and watched as the screaming soldiers fled from the burning trucks. Unsure of where to run for cover, the distressed Germans were easy targets for Jewish snipers.

Yet the Germans made significant gains when, shortly thereafter, General Stroop began to make good on his threat to burn the Jews out of the ghetto. The offensive began in the brushmakers' district as truckloads of Nazis drove in, placed gasoline barrels in front of the stores and apartment buildings, and ignited the explosive containers.

Within minutes, the entire area became a fiery death trap. As the flames spread, escape from the surrounding buildings became extremely treacherous. Suddenly, from out of nowhere, hundreds of Jews emerged from their hot, smoke-filled bunkers. A number of these less-than-sturdy structures had begun to cave in from the heat. Many badly burned individuals who reached the street hoping to surrender were immediately gunned down by the Nazis. In other cases, Jews overcome by the flames or smoke inhalation died before they could find their way out.

One bunker in which a number of ZOB fighters had sought refuge lost its exit after a Nazi grenade destroyed the steps leading down to the cellar. Although flames spanned the floor above, the fighters placed a board across the burning expanse, on which they hoped to walk to safety. They dampened their shirts and held the water-soaked cloth to their faces to fend off the heat, smoke, and flames as they tried to make their way out of the bunker. The dense black smoke made it difficult for the fighters to see ahead, and burning rafters seemed to fall wherever they walked.

Somehow the small group reached the outdoors, where the fire's intense heat had turned the pavement to a hot sticky substance that clung to the soles of their shoes. They rested momentarily in a courtyard while devising a plan to get to the central ghetto. The rebels sent out a two-person patrol to look for possible routes, but their scouts soon returned with a grim appraisal of the situation. They could either pass through an area filled with armed German soldiers or allow the flames that now nearly consumed the brushmakers' district to catch up with them. Deciding to brave the Germans' firepower, the group headed for the central ghetto. Amazingly, all but one reached their destination.

Death seemed to encompass the brushmakers' district as Stroop's plan to smoke out the hidden Jews proved to be even more effective than he had anticipated. Yet although the Nazis attained their highest number of casualties by setting the buildings on fire, not everyone was forced from the bunkers. The ZZW headquarters, stationed in an extremely well ventilated and solidly constructed bunker, remained intact through all the chaos.

Unfortunately, all the rebel forces were not comparably protected. Before long, the fire scorching the brushmakers' district spread to the central ghetto, where significant numbers of ZOB fighters had been attempting to battle the Nazis. When the hideaway out of which the ZOB had largely operated was destroyed, Mordechai Anielewicz regretted his decision not to construct rebel bunkers for fear of weakening the group's fighting spirit. Stranded in the midst of a burning ghetto, Anielewicz had become a commander without a command post. He realized that his fighters would now be at the mercy of terrified civilians to shield them within the remaining bunkers. He vowed to persevere, but feared that if his organization fragmented, the rebellion would be over.

A resistance fighter jumps from a burning building to avoid being captured by Nazi soldiers.

CHAPTER 6

The Battle Continues

With portions of the ghetto now in ruins, General Stroop had begun to achieve the results he had hoped for. Yet he was still not entirely satisfied with his men's performance. Although the brushmakers' district experienced considerable devastation, the Nazis had not been able to capture ZZW headquarters, and the Polish and Zionist flags still flew as reminders to the Germans that the rebellion continued.

However, ZZW defense forces were significantly dissipated by the Nazi attacks. German artillery had destroyed one of the machine guns next to the flags flying from the rooftop of their headquarters, and a number of the fighters had been either killed or wounded in skirmishes with the enemy. Those left were exhausted from fighting and from continually having to be on the alert for Nazi attacks.

At that point, ZZW leaders determined that their only

hope of inflicting additional Nazi casualties was to draw the German soldiers into an ambush at their headquarters. To lure them into the trap, the rebels pretended that their organization had been completely destroyed in the fire. They took down the machine gun remaining on the roof, but left up the two flags as a challenge to the Nazis to remove them. Then the rebel fighters hid, clutching their weapons as they waited for the Germans to take the bait.

At first the Nazis didn't budge, but after about fifteen minutes, several German officers met in a doorway across the street from the rebel headquarters to determine how to proceed. The ZZW then attempted one of its most brazenly daring moves. A blond, blue-eyed rebel wearing a stolen Nazi officer's uniform approached the Germans from a back exit so that they had no way of knowing that he'd come from the enemy post. Convinced that the Jewish rebel was actually a German officer who had bravely ventured ahead to check on the situation, the Nazis agreed to follow him up a staircase to ZZW headquarters. The duped officers felt certain that this was their chance to remove the enraging rooftop rebel flags and win General Stroop's approval.

But as soon as he reached the first landing, the disguised ZZW fighter swiftly darted to an open window and threw a grenade at the enemy soldiers about to follow him inside. The other Jewish fighters stationed at various windows throughout the building simultaneously dropped their grenades and fired at the Germans below. Quite a few enemy soldiers fell before the survivors were able to find refuge on a nearby street.

Stroop, infuriated by the incident, sent back a special SS task force to finally remove the flags and destroy any ZZW rebels who were still alive. To ensure the operation's success,

Stroop had one of his most-decorated SS officers, First Lieutenant Otto Dehmke, head the force. However, the honored Nazi lieutenant turned out to be among the first Germans to perish in the assault. A grenade he had intended for the Jews exploded in his hand after he was hit by a rebel bullet.

Upon receiving word of the attack's failure and the loss of one of his favorite officers, General Stroop grew incensed. He immediately ordered that 120 Jews be rounded up and shot in retaliation for Lieutenant Dehmke's death. He also became determined to harden his policy against Warsaw's Jews. Although he had warned the German businessmen that he could not safeguard their factories and supply houses, he had actually attempted to avoid these areas in burning out Jewish civilians and rebels. Now he felt that he could no longer afford to be so cautious.

Later that day, the Nazis torched a number of buildings near ZZW headquarters. Soon flames consumed the street as the air filled with dust and smoke. Before long, a sickening stench arose—it was the combined odor of charred human flesh and building materials. Although the sound of German artillery roared throughout the area, the screams of people being burned alive in the hideouts could still be heard.

Many Jews who had been hiding in hallways and apartments either jumped from the torched buildings or were burned to death. Some who had pistols vainly tried to fire on the Germans below, while others fell to their deaths shouting protest slogans such as "Down with the Nazis." Some individuals tried to break their falls by first throwing down mattresses or pillows to land on. However, few survived, since German marksmen surrounding the building usually picked them off before they reached the ground.

Some quickly swallowed vials of poison they kept with

them to avoid a more torturous death at the hands of the Germans. But with the fire rapidly spreading, they now feared that the flames might reach them before the poison took effect. And unfortunately, even those who took poison did not always die painlessly.

One man had the misfortune of swallowing a defective bottle of poison, which resulted in an excruciatingly slow, painful end. When a group of Nazis found him tormented on the ground, he begged them to shoot him to end his misery. But although the soldiers had been scavenging the ghetto, shooting Jews who'd escaped from the burning rubble, they refused to kill the dying man. Instead they threw his body on a pile of corpses and laughed as he slowly died.

Other Jews who escaped found that the German soldiers now hunted them as though they were wild beasts. To discover any bunkers they might have missed, the enemy had even brought in dogs and sound-detection equipment.

The Jews they rounded up who weren't immediately killed were taken to the deportation area. Some were in incredible pain after having been badly burned while exiting their buildings. One young mother's hands and arms were too severely charred to pick up her small child. Others, who'd been burned beyond recognition, lay on the floor screaming in pain.

The German guards watching over them were indiscriminately cruel in their treatment of the captives. Anyone might be hit over the head with a rifle butt for no apparent reason, while a number of Jewish girls, who were little more than children, were raped and beaten. Some guards made groups of elderly Jewish men dance prior to shooting them in the head. Even the Judenrat leaders, whom many felt had sold out their people to make things easier for themselves, were gathered together for their final due. Four of them were lined up against a wall and shot.

As the ghetto fires spread, the ZZW rebels were finally forced to leave their headquarters. Unfortunately, bands of well-armed German soldiers were waiting for them outside. Some were gunned down on the spot, while others were taken to the railroad for deportation. But several ZZW leaders, along with a number of the fighters, managed to escape in the chaos. Finding temporary shelter wherever they could, the group leaders attempted to contact the scattered ZZW factions. As they no longer felt able to carry on the ghetto struggle, members were encouraged to escape through the previously dug tunnels and join the partisans fighting the enemy in the forests.

But leaving the ghetto would not be as easy as they had hoped, since the Germans had discovered many of the secret passageways leading to the gentile side of Warsaw. Several ZZW rebels who tried to go were stopped by the Nazis before they had even gotten halfway through the tunnels. To use the smallest number of soldiers to prevent tunnel escapes, Stroop had many of these underground passages filled with water or gas. This way, fleeing Jews either drowned or died of asphyxiation before they could reach safety.

One ZZW fighter found a working telephone in the basement of a ghetto factory and called a contact on the gentile side to ask for help. This had been his last hope, and he was bitterly disappointed to hear that the ghetto was now too closely guarded for the Home Army to assist the Jews. It was a sad time for the brave ZZW rebel, who had hoped to go on fighting. His group's desperation was further underscored when the fighters looked up to see that the Nazis had finally taken down the flags representing their people's freedom and future.

Of course, some ghetto fighters and civilians still tried to escape. One civilian group used an underground tunnel the Nazis hadn't discovered yet and emerged on Warsaw's gentile side after lifting up a manhole cover. But they had little time to rejoice, since moments later a gang of informers descended on them. The Jews temporarily bought their way out of the situation by offering the men all their money, but their freedom was soon over. Less than an hour later, they were turned in by another informer, who had received a handsome sum from the Germans.

However, Mordechai Anielewicz and a number of other ZOB fighters had miraculously survived the last few days of fighting and were determined to continue. Perhaps surprisingly, their new headquarters were to be set up in the ghetto's largest and best-equipped remaining bunker—the hideout of a gang of thieves and smugglers who had become wealthy in the ghetto's early days. Now faced with possible capture and deprived of any money-making ventures, they welcomed the armed rebels to their bunker. As their spokesperson related to Anielewicz: "Whatever is ours is yours, and we are at your disposal. We are alert, and agile, and well trained in breaking locks, in sneaking silently and unnoticed in the night, and in climbing fences and walls. And we are well acquainted with all the paths and holes in the destroyed ghetto. You will see that we will be useful to you."[1] The idealistic young rebels had teamed up with the ghetto outlaws. It seemed an unlikely match, but one that might prove useful to what remained of Warsaw's Jews.

As Mordechai Anielewicz surveyed the luxuriously immense bunker he now occupied, he could scarcely believe that such accommodations still existed in the ghetto. Before their arrival, less than 50 people had shared the bunker,

One of the many hiding places
scattered throughout the ghetto

which was equipped with electricity, a full-service kitchen, plush sofas, and a recreation room.

In the comfort and safety of his new hideaway, the ZOB leader had an opportunity to send a note to Yitzhak Zuckerman, his organization's deputy in Warsaw's gentile sector, who was still actively trying to procure arms for the rebels. Anielewicz stressed the urgent need for grenades, automatic weapons, and explosives with which to construct bombs. He explained that pistols were only of limited use to them, since the rebels could too easily be downed by Nazi artillery before reaching the range within which a pistol could hit its mark. He urged Zuckerman to continue to try to buy arms, but added that at least the Warsaw Jews had bravely fought the Nazis, and he would die knowing that his people did not blindly follow their murderers to the slaughter.

Mordechai Anielewicz's message reached Yitzhak Zuckerman through one of the bunker's smugglers who still managed to maintain contacts on the other side of the wall. Zuckerman had not made very much headway in persuading Christian Poles to support the ghetto Jews, and now felt that he needed to resort to more inflammatory tactics. Zuckerman printed up a manifesto designed to incite rebellion among gentile Poles and distributed these materials both to members of the Polish underground and to the general population. The leaflet advocated what the Germans feared most—a show of Polish solidarity through a united armed resistance. Urging "death to the hangmen and killers," Zuckerman stressed that they must join together to win back their country from the invaders.

Unfortunately, the incendiary flyer fell into the hands of General Stroop, who was outraged by the Jewish rebels' attempts to actively enlist gentile Polish support. His annoyance was heightened by a cable he'd just received from Himmler, conveying the high command's displeasure with the prolonged ghetto resistance and calling for swifter, tougher measures in dealing with the Jews.

General Stroop decided that he needed to be even firmer with the rebels than he had been in the last few days. Now he arranged for German aircraft to bomb ghetto areas believed to be rebel strongholds. He also issued a decree prohibiting Polish civilians from entering the ghetto for any reason. Gentile Poles found there were to be shot on sight. To show that he intended to severely punish anyone assisting Jews, Stroop had an entire Christian family publicly shot for having hidden a Jewish child.

Yet, a limited number of Christian Poles wanted to help the Jewish rebels despite Stroop's sinister threats. A unit of the Home Army, acting on its own, attacked several small SS patrols near the Jewish cemetery and at other ghetto sites. But even though these Poles had risked their lives, only two German soldiers were killed, and the rebels were still left to fight largely on their own.

Stroop's destruction of various ghetto areas made communication between surviving ZOB units extremely difficult. Rebel battle stations in the productive ghetto tried to keep in touch with one another through a young ZOB agent named Regina Fuden. With her long, blond, curly hair and radiant smile, Fuden was like a breath of fresh air to those who depended on her nightly visits to the rebel posts in cellars, attics, and blocked-off rooms. She provided a sense of continuity by bringing both orders and news reports to soldiers united in a common cause who hadn't seen one another in days. Often called their "visiting angel," Regina was both brave and determined. She always insisted on making her

A housing block in the ghetto is destroyed as the Nazis try to burn the Jews out of their hiding places.

CHAPTER 7

The Burning Ghetto

The unextinguished fires set by the Nazis continued to burn through the ghetto, and within days, nearly every bunker in the central ghetto had been scorched. The effects were disastrous both for the thousands of concealed civilians in the district as well as for the many scattered ZOB fighting units that were not with Mordechai Anielewicz's group in the well-insulated smugglers' bunker.

As seas of people emerged from their hot, smoke-filled hideouts, the rebels, who'd also been forced out into the street, tried to organize the crowd and assist them in finding new hiding places. But it was nearly impossible to maintain order in the panicked group, which seemed to grow larger by the minute.

Carrying whatever they could salvage from their bunkers, people pushed their way into the fleeing throng. They pressed forward, hoping to survive, but their prospects were poor. The hundreds of ZOB rebels within the human throng faced little better odds. Now they were fighting units without either an operational base or an action plan. The rebels were ill-prepared to rescue anyone at this time, but the civilians begged the fighters to save them.

The fighters realized that when the Nazis could not stop the rebellion with bullets, grenades, and bombs, they would again resort to fire to drive the Jews out. Hope in the ghetto was rapidly slipping away. Without food, water, weapons, and ammunition, how were the rebels to defend their people?

The Jewish fighters talked among themselves, trying to devise a new plan. Among those leading the discussion was ZOB fighter Ziuvia Lubetkin, whose husband, Yitzhak Zuckerman, was still on the gentile side trying to secure weapons for the rebels and encouraging Christian Poles to join the fight. As she looked up at the smoke-filled sky and listened to the sound of Nazi artillery in the background, she wondered if she'd ever see her husband again.

But moments later, a young civilian approached the fighters to tell them about a sewer tunnel leading to the gentile side that the Nazis didn't know about. Lubetkin and the others wondered if small groups of Jews could find their way through the tunnel and escape to the other side. Remaining safe in the gentile district was certainly an unlikely prospect. But things had deteriorated to the point that no possibility could be ruled out.

The group decided that the following morning, four Aryan-looking rebels would test the escape route. If they made it through, they could contact Yitzhak Zuckerman to see if evacuation plans could be made for larger numbers of Jews. In the meantime, they could only try to hide from the Nazis until the trial run to the gentile side the next day.

While Jewish rebels and civilians in the central ghetto desperately searched for a way to survive, Stroop focused his full attention on the productive ghetto. Threatening to use aerial bombs, the general loudly announced that if the Jews didn't come out at once, their bunkers would be blown up. A large number of civilians decided to surrender, but the ZOB rebels in the area remained in hiding. They were determined to continue fighting, although at the moment, there was little they could do to hamper the enemy.

The rebels saw German soldiers leading civilians to deportation areas, but couldn't open fire on them for fear of hitting the Jews. They could only look on as their friends and neighbors were led away and wonder if this was the end of their people.

With the Jewish resistance no longer the threat it had previously been, Stroop allowed his men's destruction of the ghetto to continue after dark. By early evening, the general had returned to the central ghetto, where his troops continued to use fire to root out those Jews who had found new hiding places after being smoked out of their original bunkers. Stroop gleefully looked on as his men ravaged the central ghetto, unmercifully murdering the Jews whose resistance had become a source of embarrassment to their commander. Now 24 armed units used both gas and grenades, in addition to fire, to drive the fugitives from the bunkers they had missed earlier that day.

Stroop even considered honoring the officer who eventually demolished the most bunkers with a special battlefield decoration. Yet as he watched them work, he felt that many men deserved recognition. In Stroop's mind, they were the true Nazi heroes—to hasten the ghetto's cleanup, they'd shot the women and children fleeing from the fire as though they were rats scurrying from a pantry.

By then the Nazis' fun in destroying the ghetto seemed relentless. Yet on Easter Sunday, despite the blazing fires and death screams emanating from the ghetto, a festive holiday atmosphere prevailed in gentile Warsaw. Dressed in their best spring outfits, the Christian Poles strolled down the city streets, chatting with their friends and neighbors and playing with their children in the warm, bright sunlight.

While some Poles carefully avoided the ghetto-wall area, others seemed drawn to it. From there they could witness the Nazis' ongoing destruction of the ghetto. Even though the scenes were horrific, some people lifted their small children in the air so that they wouldn't miss seeing Jews on fire jump to their deaths from ghetto buildings.

General Stroop was in good humor that Easter morning. He had admiringly watched his men kill ghetto Jews until about two o'clock in the morning, and after a good night's sleep, he was determined to enjoy a tasty Easter meal before returning to the battle site.

While the German SS general dined, four rebels in Ziuvia Lubetkin's ZOB unit entered the sewer tunnel leading to the manhole they hoped to escape through to reach Warsaw's Christian district. It was a risky operation, but the fighters had little to lose, since at any time they could be killed by the German soldiers who were carefully combing the ghetto for Jews.

As they entered the dank tunnel, the rebels saw hundreds of terrified civilians clinging to life in the excrement and other sewer filth that characterized their underground environment. They were frightened and hungry, and many had been wounded through encounters with the enemy. Although some in the tunnel had died, there hadn't been a way to remove the bodies without attracting the attention of the Nazi soldiers they hid from. As it turned out, the bodies were often carried away by the motion of the sewer water.

After hours of pushing through the densely packed crowd, the four ZOB fighters finally reached their destination. But just as they were about to lift the manhole cover, they heard German voices above them. The rebels waited until they thought it was safe before the first two climbed out. But no sooner were they standing on solid ground than they were cornered and captured by a group of Polish policemen who immediately turned them over to the Germans.

The third Jewish rebel, who was about to emerge, quickly darted back into the tunnel, but before he could close the manhole cover a German bullet grazed his cheek. The rebels realized that the Nazis had become aware of many more of the ghetto's escape routes and that this particular sewer opening was among the most well guarded spots in Warsaw. Jewish refugees could no longer leave the ghetto that way. Now the rebels would have to protect themselves as well as they could while looking for another way out for their people.

General Stroop's plan to burn the Jews out of their hiding places had been extremely effective. But even though the Nazis were assured of a resounding victory in the ghetto, Stroop felt that the process had already taken too long. He wanted to complete the task as soon as possible and hoped to encircle the entire ghetto with a ring of fire, leaving only a narrow strip of territory intact. If everything went according to plan, the Jews would collect themselves for Nazi disposal by flocking to this small island of safety. He would rely on antiaircraft guns and other forms of heavy artillery to ensure that the rebels did not find some other unanticipated escape means through which to thwart his final efforts to dissolve the ghetto.

Stroop believed his scheme would work, but he was concerned that once nearly the entire ghetto was in flames, he would have to contend with the simultaneous surrender of tens of thousands of Jews. If that occurred, he doubted that he had sufficient manpower to handle the teeming masses. Stroop also knew that the deportation area was already overflowing with Jews waiting for trains. The general realized that it was imperative to streamline the influx of Jewish prisoners to a manageable number. Therefore, that Easter Sunday, Stroop's SS units were told to kill as many Jews as possible in preparation for the large-scale action.

The Nazis were quite methodical in proceeding with the Easter mass murders. It was determined that Pawiak Prison, situated within the ghetto, would make an excellent execution site. Early that morning, German guards shepherded Jewish men, women, and children who had either surrendered or been captured to the prison. By that afternoon, the line of prisoners extended as far as the eye could see.

As space permitted, the Jews were led into the prison courtyard and ordered to lie flat on the ground. The SS guards then brought small groups of between five and ten prisoners to another courtyard down the street, which was surrounded by abandoned buildings. There would be a ripple of gunfire, the sound of screams, and then silence. After SS guards had stacked the bodies into a neat pile, the next group was brought in.

Back at the courtyard, the terrified captives awaited their turn while contemplating how many minutes they had left to live. Some walked to their deaths solemnly, perhaps clasping the hand of a friend or a loved one, while others begged and pleaded with their Nazi escorts for mercy. But in either case, none escaped the fate the SS had planned for them that day.

Unaware of Ziuvia Lubetkin's group's foiled sewer escape to the gentile district, Mordechai Anielewicz now regretted that he had been against digging underground tunnels out of the ghetto. All the telephones in the area were dead, and it seemed nearly impossible to reach Yitzhak Zuckerman or any other ZOB contacts on the gentile side who might be able to raise support for the movement. The ZOB rebels thought that perhaps their only chance now rested in an ironic consequence of the Nazi fires. Stroop had tried to preserve one ghetto factory considered especially important to Germany's war effort, and when the flames reached that structure, he called in Polish firemen to extinguish the blaze. Mordechai Anielewicz hoped that one of the fire fighters could be bribed into helping them get in touch with their contacts in gentile Warsaw.

But unfortunately, the Polish firemen treated the Jews with such disdain that the rebels doubted that they would be of any help. One fire fighter stood chuckling as the flames licked the shoes of a man holding a small child on the balcony of a burning building. In a moment he would be forced to jump into a fiery pit or be consumed by the rapidly approaching flames. Although the fire fighter observing this scene was holding a powerful water hose, he made no attempt to douse the burning area surrounding the Jewish man and child. Instead he yelled up to the balcony, "Throw your valuables down to me before you jump." But the cornered man chose not to comply with the request. He merely spat on the fireman before he and the child jumped to their deaths.

Jewish department heads of an armament factory are arrested by Nazi soldiers.

CHAPTER 8

Hope and Sorrow

Although General Stroop had counted on demolishing what remained of the ghetto after more than a week of fighting, the operation had not proceeded swiftly enough for him to maintain his self-imposed deadline. More Jews would have to be rooted out and murdered to prevent intense overcrowding when the ghetto was finally leveled.

Among those still to be killed were the Jewish police officers who had assisted the Nazis in their brutal oppression of Warsaw's Jewish population. Having accumulated some wealth through the bribes offered them by desperate others, many of the men had hoped to survive the war and live comfortably on their ill-gotten gains. But now they discovered that the Germans intended to murder them along with the other Jews. They had sold out their own people for nothing.

The Jewish police force was soon assembled in the ghetto, where a Nazi officer greeted them and thanked them for their service. The policemen were then marched under armed guard to the courtyard at the prison where the mass executions had previously taken place. The victims realized that it was pointless to beg for mercy. They hadn't shown any in carrying out their duties, and knew that none would be forthcoming for them now. Following the executions, the police officers' bodies, along with the preceding day's corpses, were placed in two emptied factory buildings that were set on fire.

As the Jewish policemen were executed, Nazi soldiers in other ghetto areas continued to hunt for and kill Jews in hiding. Civilian Jews grew increasingly desperate as they saw the Nazi forces closing in on them. That day a group of about thirty friends and neighbors had just relocated to their third bunker after having been burned out of their first two hideouts. But just hours after they arrived, they began to smell smoke and hear quickly paced footsteps above them. And when an infant in the bunker started to cry, the others warned the child's parents to quiet the baby before the sound revealed their whereabouts.

Once the parents realized that they couldn't calm the infant, the father handed a nurse among them a hypodermic needle filled with an unknown substance and asked her to inject the child. After she refused, the father did it himself, and the baby finally fell asleep. Shortly afterward, the bunker occupants realized that the footsteps they heard had not been Nazi boots, but the sound of Jews fleeing the flames around them. When the baby's parents later tried to wake their child, they were unable to. Horrified, they realized that their infant son was dead because of a terrible mistake.

A number of ZOB fighters perished in skirmishes as Nazi grenades forced them to abandon their protective hiding posts. The rebels were keenly aware of the number of bullets they had left. At this stage of the battle it was especially important not to waste ammunition—and to make certain that a single bullet remained for them in case they were captured.

Many of the fighters—along with the civilians who clung to them—now headed for Mordechai Anielewicz's bunker, since their own hiding places had been demolished by the Nazis. By sundown, the once spacious, well-equipped hideout overflowed with more than 300 people. It was impossible to pass through the hallways, where people were so tightly packed together that they could hardly breathe. As there was just a single toilet, many of the occupants were forced to relieve themselves where they stood, adding to their humiliation and despair.

Mordechai Anielewicz tried to keep his fighters' spirits up, but everyone knew the rebellion was in its last stages. The Germans were closing in around them, ammunition and supplies were low, and no assistance appeared to be forthcoming from the gentile Poles.

Isolated in their bunker, these ZOB rebels had no way of knowing that help would actually spring from an unexpected source in the ghetto itself. It was initially thought that the ZZW, the other rebel fighting group, had been demolished in the early days of battle. Although the organization had lost a good deal of manpower to Nazi fire, a number of the fighters—including the group's founder, David Appelbojm—had escaped. The small group had spent the last few days devising a plan that would permit a large number of Jews to leave the ghetto through still another underground tunnel. However, these ZZW leaders knew that once the Nazis became aware of a large-scale exodus of Jews, the fighters would need weapons and ammunition to keep the enemy at bay, and these items were in short supply.

That day, the ZZW managed to enhance the rebels' weapon supply by stealing some of what they needed from the German ghetto forces. Wearing stolen SS uniforms, two rebel brothers passed as German officers as they pushed their sister through the streets, loudly cursing and insulting her. It was a common-enough scene, since the Germans often degraded their victims after capturing them. But instead of taking their sister to the assembly area for deportation, the three walked straight into the SS supply facility and started shooting. The guards were startled by the attack and weren't sure who the enemy was, since nearly everyone present wore an SS uniform. As the Germans shot at one another, the Jewish family gathered several boxes of guns and bullets. Additional ZZW fighters immediately arrived at the scene to collect the fallen Germans' weapons.

Although delighted with what they'd accumulated that day, ZZW leaders knew that much more was needed. To contact the Polish Home Army officers who'd assisted them in the past, two ZZW rebels safely used the tunnel that the organization hoped scores of Jews would escape through. After delivering the message, the men could scarcely believe their ears when they were told that the Polish underground would send a combat unit into the ghetto to supply the ZZW with what was needed. Home Army captain Iwanski, who had always supported the ZZW, regardless of his organization's stand, looked forward to entering the ghetto to help the Jewish fighters. He collected a wagonload of weapons, which were packed in burlap sacks and fastened to the backs of the captain and the 17 Polish underground volunteers accompanying him on this important mission. Among those in Iwanski's combat unit were his two brothers and his 16-year-old son.

Besides the 18 men entering the ghetto, a band of about 60 others—which included both Home Army fighters and ZZW rebels already in the gentile sector—remained behind to ensure that the tunnel stayed open at that end. They would also help the Jewish refugees returning with the Poles to find sanctuaries.

Iwanski and his men came safely through the tunnel, where they were met by the ZZW leaders expecting them. But there was little time for pleasantries, since a Jewish messenger immediately approached them to report that the Germans were on their way. Nazi troop movement had been spotted in the vicinity, and moments later the rebel fighters could hear the rumble of trucks and tanks. With the Nazis about to strike, the Christian Poles decided to remain and help the ZZW battle the enemy even though they had only promised to deliver the weapons and escort Jewish civilians back through the sewer tunnel.

Unfortunately, things did not go well for the rebel forces, as they unexpectedly found themselves up against a massive display of German firepower. They were showered with a continuing barrage of mortar shells, while aircraft bomber pilots stalked them from above. The small rebel fighting group actually never had a chance, since hours before the attack, a traitor had informed the Nazis that the Polish underground would be assisting ghetto Jews. Determined to flatten what he thought could be the beginning of a gentile Polish revolt, Stroop struck the rebels with unprecedented forcefulness.

The results were disastrous; the Nazis refused to retreat until nearly every rebel had been wounded or killed. When it was over, the Germans sent ambulances to the battle site to collect their wounded, but the rebels were left without proper medical care, supplies, or even a safe place to rest.

Captain Iwanski was hit by a bullet in the head, and it was doubtful that he would survive without medical attention. ZZW founder David Appelbojm had been shot twice and was rapidly losing blood. In their present condition, Iwanski realized, it would be impossible for the rebels to lead significant numbers of civilians out of the ghetto. He urged Appelbojm and the other surviving ZZW fighters to accompany him and his men through the tunnel to a safe place where they could regain their strength.

But while some of the Jewish fighters were grateful for the captain's offer, Appelbojm refused to go. Although he'd always planned to exit the ghetto to fight outside its perimeters with the Polish underground, now he felt unable to leave his people to die while he saved himself. He wished Iwanski and those accompanying him well and asked them to be sure to let the world know of the Nazi atrocities in the ghetto and how the Jews valiantly fought to the end. Iwanski promised to do so, and he also said that he'd try to launch another operation to bring out the civilians. Then, along with almost 50 fighters, he left through the tunnel. When they reached the other side, they were taken to a Polish underground hospital on the outskirts of town. Later that evening, David Appelbojm died in the ghetto.

Unknown to the ZZW or Captain Iwanski, some ZOB rebels in another part of the ghetto had begun to reevaluate their initial fighting philosophy. Now they felt that it was better to fight the Nazis outside the ghetto than to perish defending an unsavable area, and planned to escape through still another tunnel. The group was to be led by Regina Fuden, whose nightly visits to various ZOB fighting posts as the organization's liaison had made her familiar with every possible escape path.

Although the ZZW had not established a hospital for its wounded ghetto soldiers, these ZOB rebels had tried to bring their wounded fighters to a small room hidden from the enemy by a trapdoor. They never had sufficient supplies, but whenever possible, they brought in a Jewish ghetto doctor to treat those injured. The rebels also fed and sponge-bathed the fallen fighters and tried to make them as comfortable as possible.

But as the ZOB fighters contemplated escaping through the tunnel, they faced a difficult decision. How could they leave their wounded comrades behind? Many of those injured could barely stand or walk, and since the attic passageways had been nearly demolished by the enemy, the rebels would have to scale buildings, jump from one rooftop to the next, and duck the Germans' bullets just to reach the tunnel.

Abandoning their wounded fellow fighters was extremely difficult. They couldn't tell them that anyone left behind would probably soon die from a Nazi bullet or be burned alive. Yet even though the wounded hadn't left the room for days, the rebels caring for them thought they might have guessed what was really happening outside. Some continually asked if that burning smell (the odor of burning buildings) was coming closer. After saying their good-byes, the unit leader promised that, although they would not be coming back, someone would stay to care for them.

Once outside, he ordered one of the female fighters to remain behind to cook for the wounded and change their bandages. However, the young woman resisted, arguing that her dying with the wounded would not change their fate. She accused the unit leader of selecting her because she was a woman and stressed that she'd already proven herself an able fighter.

The group's leader found himself facing a perplexing moral dilemma. He certainly didn't want to sacrifice the young fighter's life, but felt he couldn't leave the injured unassisted. As it turned out, he never had to make that decision, since another woman in the group volunteered to stay. She felt she had little to live for because her fiancé, who was also a fighter, had already been murdered by the Nazis. The young woman urged the others to hurry on ahead, as timing was crucial to their escape. She was content to care for those left behind and die with them as well.

Meanwhile, the German industrialists who owned factories in the ghetto had grown increasingly anxious. They had been unable to convince a sufficient number of able-bodied Jews to volunteer to staff their relocated factories and feared that at any time, Stroop might make good on his threat to burn down the entire ghetto. In retaliation for the Nazi torchings, Jewish rebels had already set fire to a number of vital factory supply centers, and the Nazi entrepreneurs felt that their businesses might soon go up in smoke if a miracle didn't occur.

Mordechai Anielewicz, along with other ZOB members in the overcrowded bunker, also hoped for a miracle. Requesting assistance in their struggle from every possible source, Mordechai drafted a plea to the exiled Polish government in London, explaining the full impact of Nazi devastation and genocide and stressing that only the intervention of the Allied forces could save them now:

> Artillery and flamethrowers are employed and airplanes shower high explosives and incendiary bombs on the forty thousand Jews who still remain in the ghetto. The Germans mine and blast blocks of houses where the residents put up resistance. . . .

Only the power of the Allied nations can offer immediate and active help now. On behalf of the millions of Jews murdered and burned alive, on behalf of those fighting back and all of us condemned to die, we call on the whole world: It is imperative that the powerful retaliation of the Allies shall fall upon the bloodthirsty enemy immediately and not in some distant future, so that it will be quite clear what the retaliation is for. . . .[1]

Once the rebels managed to smuggle the letter to a contact in the Polish underground, they felt sure it would be speedily delivered. Unfortunately, the message did not reach London until nearly a month after the ghetto had been completely demolished.

Wealthy Jews living outside the ghetto are rounded up by German officials.

CHAPTER 9

The Last Stages

As May Day (May 1) dawned in the ghetto, Mordechai Anielewicz and his ZOB fighters decided to mark this spring holiday of rebirth with a display of renewed fighting zeal. These fighters expected to die, and their low ammunition supply seriously limited any damage they were capable of inflicting on German forces. Yet Anielewicz was determined that things would be different on May Day: They would stage the most dramatic assault against the Nazis that they were capable of. The fighters didn't know if they would survive the attack, but they viewed fighting back on May Day as perhaps their last show of strength and determination.

The rebels watched for the Nazis to approach as they squatted near the windows of a burned-out ghetto building. Soon they heard the sound of German voices, and moments later saw a Jewish informer point out a structure in which some Jews still hid. Before entering the building, one of the

Nazi officers took out his pistol and shot their Jewish guide. But just as he fell to the ground, the hidden rebels began firing on the Nazi soldiers. Three were hit and the others immediately fled, astounded to find that the Jewish rebels were still capable of mounting an offensive. They returned within the hour, but by then the Jews had found an even better vantage point from which to shoot, and inflicted greater Nazi casualties than before.

Reports of the Jewish fighters' attack served to undermine Stroop's image and authority. Renewed rebel action made the general look especially bad at this point, since he'd already informed his superiors that the rebel strongholds had been largely dissipated. Still not prepared to burn down the entire ghetto, Stroop consulted with a street-fighting specialist from the SS special-operations branch on how to best disarm the rebels. This man suggested that small, late-night patrols of well-armed SS men especially trained in guerrilla warfare be sent into the ghetto to detect and destroy any remaining rebel hideouts.

Stoop immediately set about organizing the new SS patrols, yet he remained especially troubled by the recent unpleasant turn of events. The Nazi party had convinced Stroop that Jews were subhumans who were actually more like animals than people. But if this were so, the general wondered why it took such large numbers of Germans to defeat them.

Stroop also felt dismayed after witnessing the rebels' bravery and perseverance on numerous occasions. Just that afternoon, Stroop had looked on as his men continued to round up Jews for deportation and execution. Suddenly a young fighter who'd been caught with the others unexpectedly drew out a pistol and used his last three bullets to kill a German officer standing among them.

The other Nazis immediately riddled the young fighter's body with bullets, and even Stroop managed to get in several shots before the rebel fell. The SS general arrogantly stood over the Jewish fighter, relishing this opportunity to watch him slowly die. He had expected to see pain or fear on the rebel's face, but even in his last moments of life, the ZOB fighter remained defiant. The Nazis' bloody victim struggled to raise his head and with his last breath spat on Stroop. That young Jew's daring sent a chill down the general's spine. Stroop later wrote that although he was responsible for the deaths of many thousands of Jews, he never forgot his experience that afternoon.

After being burned out of their bunkers, many of the ZOB survivors who were not with Mordechai Anielewicz took refuge in another fairly large central-ghetto bunker. As the entrance to this bunker was extremely well disguised, the Nazis had missed it when they had burned others nearby. Yet in recent days, the bunker occupants had heard soldiers' footsteps above them and wondered how long they would remain undetected. As the Nazis continued to comb the area, it was obvious that they suspected that the rebels were hiding in the vicinity.

The Jewish fighters tried to think of the best way to handle the situation. They contemplated leaving the bunker to fight the Nazis face-to-face, but soon realized that they would probably all be killed within minutes. To increase their odds of survival, some of the rebels headed for other bunkers once nightfall came. But in the vastly burned-out ghetto, there simply wasn't adequate space for all the fighters to hide elsewhere, so most were forced to stay where they were.

Even with the departure of a portion of the rebel force,

the bunker remained quite overcrowded. But such annoyances seemed trivial that morning as the occupants silently listened to the sound of German voices directly above them.

The Nazis had discovered a woman and her kindergarten-age child hiding in a burned-out structure in the vicinity. The soldiers pulled the pair out into the courtyard and insisted that the woman tell them where the rebel fighters were hiding. When she refused, they took out a riding crop and beat her until she fell unconscious to the ground. Since she was no longer of immediate use to them, the Nazis turned to her child, who had stood behind his mother, shaking with fright.

First they offered the small boy candy to lead them to the rebels' bunker. When he refused, they used the riding crop on the child. After being whipped until he bled, the little boy gave in to them. He led the soldiers back into a burned-out building and pointed to a set of boards that could be readily pulled up. The boards covered an opening that led directly to the bunker's entrance.

Hearing what had occurred and aware that the Germans would storm the bunker momentarily, some of the rebels prepared to escape through a rear exit. It was agreed that the rebels both outside the bunker and still within would begin shooting as soon as the Nazis tried to enter. One of the older civilian men in the bunker, who didn't have a gun, decided to join the rebels. He vowed, if given the opportunity, to strangle as many Nazis as possible with his bare hands.

The rebels had a more practical plan in mind. They intended to have a beautiful young blond fighter lead the way out of the bunker's rear exit. They hoped the German soldiers might be startled by her striking good looks and therefore hesitate to shoot the seventeen-year-old. She was to enter the courtyard meekly and, while pretending to surrender, throw a grenade in the Germans' direction. It was hoped that this diversion would give the other fighters an opportunity to quickly assume strategic positions in the surrounding ruins and enable them to fight.

The tactic was somewhat successful, although several Jewish fighters were downed by German bullets as they searched for advantageous firing posts. The fray lasted several hours, and when it was over, both German and Jewish casualties were high. The rebel survivors retreated to the bunker, which the Germans had set on fire during the battle. They managed to extinguish the flames, and although the dugout was badly scorched, the fighters settled in for the night. They thought the Germans might return the following morning, but where else could a sizable number of rebels find shelter at that point?

Unfortunately, as the rebels had anticipated, their Nazi assailants returned the next morning to complete their cleanup of the rebel stronghold. The fighters felt their chances for survival were slim, but they were determined not to die without taking as many Nazis with them as possible. The rebels had planned to start shooting as soon as they could climb out of the bunker. But before they were able to exit, the Nazis threw gas bombs into the bunker, killing a significant number of those within.

Even while choking and gasping for breath, some fighters managed to crawl out of the bunker and evade the Nazi bullets aimed at them. But, most were not as fortunate. Among those killed was a sixteen-year-old boy whose parents had begged him to hide with them rather than join the ghetto's fighting forces. But the teenager had explained to them that he didn't want to spend the last days of his life crouched in fear and would rather die fighting for his people.

The youth had survived several frays, but that morning he was hit by a German bullet. Not wanting to die slowly, he handed his pistol to a fellow fighter and asked his friend to shoot him. The other fighter honored his dying comrade's last request, and moments later the brave Jewish adolescent lay dead in the street. Near him was the body of the beautiful young fighter who had been the previous day's decoy.

Despite Stroop's recent advances, the Nazi high command was still dissatisfied with his pace in eliminating the ghetto. Pressured by his superiors to finish off the rebellion, Stroop ordered an escalation of ghetto torchings and violence. Several horrified German industrialists who hadn't completed evacuating their factory equipment watched as the general's men set fire to a string of factory buildings in which he believed Jewish rebels were hiding. Stroop felt that he could no longer grant time extensions to German ghetto profiteers—ridding Warsaw of its Jews had become his chief priority, and fire was the most effective weapon to do so. As he wrote in his report of the day's activities:

> Only when the housing blocks were engulfed by fire and headed for destruction did a considerable number of Jews emerge, forced to flee the flames and smoke. . . . Others came into view on the uppermost floors at the very last moment and could save themselves from being cremated alive only by jumping. . . . Today a total number of 2,283 Jews were apprehended, of whom 204 were shot; countless Jews were destroyed in fires in the bunkers. The total sum of Jews apprehended to date has risen to 44,089.[1]

Yet, as at other times, just when it seemed as though the rebellion was doomed, help sprang from an unexpected source. As the factory fires blazed, Polish Home Army captain Iwanski—who had largely recovered from the wounds sustained in his previous ghetto battle—had begun to think of new ways to assist whatever ZZW fighters were still alive in the ghetto. Iwanski also hoped to try to rescue as many Jewish civilians as possible.

The humanitarian Polish underground captain was willing to reenter the ghetto despite the high personal and military cost of his last expedition. In addition to several outstanding fighters, the captain's brother and his sixteen-year-old son had been killed.

Nevertheless, Iwanski and another Polish underground officer now busily worked on new escape measures for the Jews. Their plan called for two small groups of Polish underground fighters to enter the ghetto through a sewer tunnel. The first band of Home Army soldiers would escort the wounded ZZW soldiers and some civilians, waiting for them near the tunnel entrance, to the gentile sector. The second Polish underground group would enter the ghetto the following night, using the same tunnel passage. They would carry weapons and ammunition to the few ZZW fighters left in the ghetto hoping to find a way to continue the rebellion.

This time, Captain Iwanski's surviving brother and his older son would accompany him on the mission. Having already lost two family members to the Nazis, Iwanski hesitated to take them along, but they insisted on coming to avenge the deaths of the others.

As the sun set, the beginning phase of Captain Iwanski's plan went into effect. The first group of Polish underground fighters successfully made their way through the sewer tunnel to find more than 100 men, women, and children eagerly awaiting their rescuers. Taking with them as many people as possible, the group started its trek back through the dark pipelike passageway. Once they reached their destination, the underground fighters began helping the others out of the tunnel at a cemetery. There the refugees were brought to safe houses in the area.

But as soon as the escapees climbed out of the tunnel, German soldiers, who had hidden behind tombstones, began shooting at them. Many of the Jews and underground fighters were killed, but some managed to escape into an adjoining cemetery, where they crouched down or lay on their stomachs for hours in the darkness until they were certain that the Germans had left. Then those who survived the Nazi attack silently headed for the sanctuaries they had been promised.

Despite the continued ghetto escapes, General Stroop's spirits had been high that day. He believed that five was his lucky number, and the SS general had frequently carried out actions against Jews in multiples of five. He would order five buildings torched, or have prisoners executed in groups of fives. Now, on May 5, Stroop's aide informed him that more than 45,000 Jews had either been captured or killed since the start of the ghetto uprising.

However, the Nazis' success did not stop the rebels and their supporters from continuing to fight. Along with his son, brother, and a number of other members of the Polish underground, Captain Iwanski began his descent into the ghetto as scheduled. As on their previous excursion, each man had a sack filled with weapons and ammunition strapped to his back to enhance the fighting capability of the remaining ZZW rebels.

When the men arrived at the predetermined spot, ZZW fighters were there to help them out of the sewer. But less than three-quarters of the Poles had emerged from the tunnel opening when the sound of barking dogs filled the air. The Nazis now regularly scoured the area with dogs, looking for hidden Jews, and apparently the canine patrol had detected Iwanski's crew.

Within seconds the Nazis were upon them, shooting at both the Jews and the Poles. Their victims tried to take cover in the surrounding burned-out buildings, hoping to return the enemy's fire. Some escaped the Nazi onslaught by quickly jumping back into the sewer. By the time the skirmish was over, a number of German soldiers were dead. But five Polish underground fighters had also been killed.

The bodies of the slain Poles were placed in sacks, and the resistance members who had hauled weapons into the ghetto now carried their dead back through the sewer. Among those killed that day were Captain Iwanski's other son and brother.

Jews burned out of their hiding places are led away by their German captors.

CHAPTER 10

A Rebellion Trampled

long with the largest surviving group of ZOB fighters, Mordechai Anielewicz remained in the hot, overcrowded bunker, contemplating the options available to them. Their food supply was nearly exhausted, and they barely had sufficient ammunition to defend themselves, let alone continue the battle with the Nazis. To worsen matters, they also strongly suspected that the Germans had discovered their bunker's general location and were likely to uncover its camouflaged entrance before long.

They hadn't imagined that just a few days earlier, Yitzhak Zuckerman and two other Jews posing as Christians in gentile Warsaw had begged the Polish underground to send a unit into the ghetto to evacuate Jewish survivors. Once again, the Home Army officers had refused, claiming that they lacked sufficient personnel, funds, and hideaways to execute such an operation.

Aware that the rebels' plight grew increasingly desperate each day, Zuckerman and his associates resorted to unorthodox methods. Pretending to be members of the Home Army, they approached a ruthless anti-Semitic smuggler, known for his ability to get the job done, and offered him a handsome sum for his help. They told the outlaw that, while working with the Jews, a number of Polish underground members had inadvertently become trapped in the ghetto. They wanted him to organize a small band of rogues to rescue these individuals. The smuggler agreed to undertake the mission on the condition that he was not asked to bring Jews out—he felt the Nazis were doing a splendid job of obliterating them.

Despite the smuggler's offensive attitude, Zuckerman and the other Jews posing as Gentiles had no compunctions about using his services or tricking him into rescuing the very people he despised. These were desperate times, and they would willingly resort to any deception to save Jewish lives.

As they planned the maneuver, Zuckerman inwardly rejoiced at the thought of seeing his wife, Ziuvia, his good friend Mordechai, and the other rebels. But within hours, his excitement turned to disappointment. The smugglers came back through the sewer empty-handed. They hadn't even been able to enter the ghetto, since Nazi patrols had been placed at all sewer openings that night. Yitzhak Zuckerman felt as though his world were caving in. He had an ominous feeling about the future, even though he didn't know that Stroop had pinpointed the exact location of Mordechai Anielewicz's bunker and intended to attack on the following day.

Early the next morning Mordechai Anielewicz and those with him in the bunker clearly heard the sound of German soldiers drilling into the elaborate wooden exterior of the entrance to their bunker directly overhead. A handful of rebels quickly left through a rear exit in the unlikely pursuit of a previously undiscovered passageway that would lead them all to safety. The other fighters drew their weapons in preparation for an attack, while some civilians shook with fear, cried, or embraced one another. But regardless of how they responded, they all knew that these were the last minutes of their lives.

Before long, a voice from outside the bunker yelled to those within, "This is your last chance. If you come out now, you'll be sent to work camps. To remain inside means death for you." But the rebels had no intention of surrendering, and one fired his rifle through the entrance in reply. An instant later, the Nazis fired back and dropped several grenades into the bunker. One German soldier began to enter the dwelling, but when he was immediately shot the others did not follow.

Instead, the Nazis began drilling substantial holes in the bunker roof. At first the civilians hoped that they would be spared, but Mordechai Anielewicz and the other fighters knew that was unlikely. Moments later, the same voice from outside again urged the occupants to surrender. The rebels responded with gunfire as they had initially, and everyone anxiously awaited the Nazis' next move.

This proved to be even worse than they had anticipated. As an unusual odor swept through the bunker, the Jews realized that the Nazis were piping in gas. While the occupants thought they might be able to dodge German bullets, they knew they would suffocate if they didn't leave.

About 100 civilians, including some of the smugglers who'd constructed the bunker, crawled out of the subterranean dwelling. Even when exposed to the fresh air, many still gasped for breath. They had left their former sanctuary reluctantly but thought that if there were any chance of their being sent to a work camp and surviving, they had to take it.

The rebels, on the other hand, had no intention of leaving the bunker. Huddled together to discuss their limited options, everyone agreed that they would not be taken alive. They knew that they were going to die, but they had resigned themselves to that fate from the rebellion's start and were surprised at having survived this long. They had done what they had set out to do—fought their people's enemy.

Some felt they should die outside while firing at the enemy. But they had only enough ammunition left to take their own lives, and if they stepped out of the bunker, the Germans might try to take the rebels alive and torture them to death.

Although suicide seemed the most expedient alternative, Anielewicz warned against acting rashly and suggested that there might be a way to counter the effects of the poisonous gas. Having heard that water neutralizes some types of gas, he asked the remaining bunker occupants to hold wet handkerchiefs to their faces. Even if only a few of them survived, there would be that many more Jews left to fight the Germans.

A few of the rebels agreed to try their leader's idea, but most decided to shoot themselves before they were too sickened by the gas to act. Shot after shot rang out as the rebels willingly extinguished their own lives. One young fighter who was unable to kill herself asked her friend and fellow fighter to shoot her. In a final gesture of fellowship, the girl's friend obliged, and then shot herself immediately afterward. Mordechai Anielewicz, who many felt embodied the rebellion's spirit, died in a corner near the water faucet, with a wet rag still on his face. The core of the rebellion had been trampled out, and there seemed to be no one left to carry on.

But less than an hour later, two ZOB rebels came bounding into the room where the mass suicides had occurred. They had been among those sent to search for new passageways when the rebels had first heard the Germans outside their bunker. Now they had returned to tell the others that a narrow tunnel existed that would lead them from the bunker, unseen by the enemy. Unfortunately, they arrived too late, and their glad tidings could not help a room of corpses.

These scouts weren't the only ones shocked by the horrifying turn of events. Some ZOB fighters from another unit, including Ziuvia Lubetkin, Marek Edelman, and others, risked a dangerous trip through the ghetto to Mordechai Anielewicz's bunker to report on how ZOB rebels had failed to reach the gentile sector through the sewer tunnels.

But when they arrived at the bunker, the small group immediately knew that something was terribly wrong. The bunker's well-disguised entrance, along with the guard usually posted there, had disappeared. A disquieting feeling swept over Lubetkin when she repeated the password and got no response.

It didn't take long for them to realize that Nazi soldiers had dynamited the bunker to ensure that everyone inside died. Lubetkin and the others tried to push aside the debris to retrieve the weapons buried with the fighters, but they didn't have the strength. They walked slowly back to their bunker, feeling that the rebellion's soul had died along with those killed in the Nazi assault.

Now only a skeleton of the ZOB remained. Lubetkin switched the organization's headquarters to the bunker where she, Marek Edelman, and a small collective of rebels were stationed. With Mordechai Anielewicz dead, Lubetkin and Edelman took over the group's command. The surviving fighters were tired and depressed, but they couldn't afford to rest. If the Nazis had learned about Anielewicz's bunker, they probably knew about theirs as well, and might come for them as early as the next morning.

Deciding that they wanted to fight with the Polish partisans in the forest, the Jews knew they had to both vacate the bunker and leave the ghetto as soon as possible. By now the sewer tunnels were the only feasible exit routes, but countless Jews had been captured or killed using these tunnels to escape. Yet as the fighters felt the Nazis upon them, they knew that they had no choice. Lubetkin and Edelman sent a small group of rebels ahead to find the best route to take. Those people who were about to leave embraced those remaining behind. They could only hope that they would see one another again soon.

While the rebels tried to escape from the ghetto, the Jews in the gentile sector posing as Christians refused to give up on staging a rescue attempt. Although Yitzhak Zuckerman's team had been barred from entering the ghetto the night before, his associate, Simcha Rathajzer, was in the process of organizing a second attempt.

Accompanied by two well-paid Christian Polish guides, the small party was only partly through the tunnel when the Poles claimed that it was too dangerous to continue. But as they started to turn back, Rathajzer drew out his pistol and forced them to go on. The loyal ZOB fighter felt that he couldn't turn back, since it was now up to him to rescue the rebellion's hero, ZOB leader Mordechai Anielewicz. Such an important mission could not be compromised because of personal risk. Simcha Rathajzer did not know that Anielewicz had

Hands raised in surrender, Jews exit a bunker blown up by Nazi shelling.

died earlier that morning.

But when he finally reached his destination and found Anielewicz's bunker destroyed, his heart sank. When Rathajzer had first left the ghetto for gentile Warsaw, the rebel forces typified life, energy, and determination. Now all that was left of those valiant young people and their fighting posts were corpses, ruins, and ashes.

Believing that there was nothing more for him to do in the ghetto, Simcha Rathajzer and his paid guides climbed back into the sewer and headed for the Christian sector of the city. But before they had gotten very far, they saw a blinding white light in the sewer. Rathajzer drew his gun, thinking he had come across a Nazi patrol. But to his relief, he had actually stumbled upon a group of ZOB rebels whom he had thought were dead. They were the fighters Ziuvia Lubetkin had sent from the bunker to locate a safe tunnel out of the ghetto.

Thrilled to find some ZOB survivors, Rathajzer quickly offered the ravenously hungry rebels the fruit and hard candy he'd brought with him. Then he explained that a rescue plan to bring Jews to the gentile sector had been formulated. He and the Polish guides would lead the refugees through the sewer while trucks waiting at the tunnel opening on the other side of the wall would speedily take them to safe havens in the forests. Rathajzer sent two men to retrieve the rest of Lubetkin and Edelman's unit and bring it to a central meeting point within the sewer tunnel. The entire group would later leave the tunnel together in gentile Warsaw.

It was almost too good to be true, yet as the rescued rebels trudged through the sewer sludge and filth, they didn't experience a sense of excitement. Everyone thought about the fighters who were not with them—those who had died fighting for their people's honor and freedom. Those young people would never see the Nazis' eventual defeat or begin a new life in a land of their own. Their hopes and dreams had been destroyed along with the ghetto.

However, there was not much time to think about the past, since they soon learned that the rescue mission wasn't proceeding as smoothly as planned. When they reached their exit point, Rathajzer went on ahead to bring the trucks to the sewer opening. The others waited anxiously, but became concerned when he didn't return after several hours.

If Rathajzer were captured, what would they do? Without a safe hiding place in the gentile district, they were sure to be spotted and captured, while to return to the ghetto meant certain death. In the meantime, the rebels could only wait in the sewer as they listened to the sound of people walking, talking, and laughing above them.

A few hours later, one of Rathajzer's contacts finally managed to slip a note to the rebels through a small opening in the manhole-cover grating. The trucks would not be available until midnight. The fighters would have to wait, stooped over in the cold dark sewer, without food or water, for ten more hours.

While the rebels waited for their transport out, Simcha Rathajzer actively tried to assure their passage. This was not an easy task, since new complications seemed to arise at every turn. After the rebels were told that the trucks would arrive at midnight, the Polish partisans helping to orchestrate their evacuation decided that moving the Jews before dawn was too risky. They'd be violating the citywide curfew imposed by the Nazis, and the sound of the trucks could too readily call attention to the operation.

So later that afternoon, a second note explaining the delay was passed to the rebels. It promised that they would be picked up in the early-morning hours when the city woke up again.

The Jewish rebels readied themselves to spend the night knee-deep in sewage, wondering if they were really going to escape after all. Perhaps their apprehension reached its zenith at about eight o'clock that evening when a third message was slipped to them. Had Simcha Rathajzer and his contacts been captured or killed? Was the Polish underground telling them to return to the ghetto? Fortunately, the delivery was just a note from Yitzhak Zuckerman, who had learned that his wife, Ziuvia, was among the rebels waiting in the sewer. He assured them that they would be saved at any cost.

As the early-morning sun filtered through the manhole-cover grating, the rebels' apprehensions began to ease. They knew that before long, Simcha Rathajzer and his contacts would whisk them away to Poland's lush green forests, where they would join forces with the partisans.

In actuality, nothing could have been further from the truth. Shortly before dawn, Rathajzer had arrived at the sewer opening, where he was to meet those bringing the trucks. He had hoped to begin loading the rebels into the vehicles immediately, but two hours passed without any sign of the trucks. Rathajzer nervously paced the sidewalk as he realized that the city streets had already become too crowded to bring the Jewish fighters out of the sewer safely.

At about 9:00 A.M. one of the men who was to bring the trucks finally arrived. He explained that he had been unable to secure the vehicles as planned, but was still working on it. Rathajzer hated to disappoint those waiting below, but felt he had no choice. He passed the rebels still another note, stating that, due to unforeseen complications, they'd have to remain where they were until midnight.

The group's leaders, Ziuvia Lubetkin and Marek Edelman, found the news especially disconcerting. They suspected that the Nazis might be blowing up the manhole openings in the ghetto behind them, which meant that there was no turning back. The two also feared that if some in the group didn't get fresh air and ample food soon, they might not make it through the day. Lubetkin and Edelman relayed their fears to Simcha Rathajzer, who decided that he would have to evacuate the Jewish fighters in broad daylight, regardless of the risks involved.

Rathajzer related the urgency of the situation to the others he had worked with in planning the rescue mission. All agreed that they would have to resort to desperate measures. A local moving company was called and asked to send two trucks to a nearby address. Other Jews working for the movement on the gentile side of the wall were sent to meet the vehicles and assist in the rebels' defense if the Nazis arrived.

Although it was still a perilous operation, things began to proceed somewhat more smoothly. Only one truck arrived, but the driver agreed to cooperate after being threatened with a gun. The rescue workers immediately began constructing a makeshift barrier of boards to camouflage the rebels' move from the sewer into the truck. They worked quickly and purposefully, as though they were actually city employees doing maintenance.

Moments later, the sewer occupants began to emerge. Swiftly boarding the vehicle, they squatted down to avoid being seen. There were a few close calls. While the rebels were climbing out to the sidewalk, a Polish police officer had approached the false construction site to see what was going on. One of the Jewish rescue workers posing as a gentile Pole told him that those leaving the sewer were members of the

Polish underground returning from a Nazi sabotage mission. This successfully appealed to the officer's patriotic sentiments, and he walked on without alerting the Germans.

Just as the truck was about to depart, Lubetkin told Rathajzer that there were still some people in the tunnel. As they had all initially crowded around the tunnel opening, she had sent small bands of individuals to other parts of the sewer to allow everyone more breathing space. Because the rescuers had come for them on such short notice, there hadn't been time to bring the others.

Rathajzer felt torn about how to proceed. The truck was already tightly packed with passengers, and he feared that the Nazis might appear at any moment. If he took the time necessary to send scouts into the sewer to search for the others, he might be jeopardizing the lives of everyone involved in the operation. Rathajzer signaled the truck to leave. If it was at all possible, he would return for the others later.

After what seemed like a very long drive, the truck finally reached its destination. The weary passengers had battled Germans for so long that at first they felt oddly out of place in the quiet fragrance of the forest. Some broke down and cried for the first time in months, while others just smiled and warmly hugged one another. They had done all they could for their people in the ghetto and had survived to continue fighting the Nazis.

While the others rejoiced in their new sense of safety and freedom, Rathajzer sent two ZOB members and a truck to rescue those who had been left behind in the sewer that morning. But when they didn't return after several hours, he went to the sewer himself to learn what had transpired. As he approached the area, he saw a crowd hovering over the bodies of the two ZOB men. His heart sank as he pondered the fate of those in the sewer.

Someone standing near Rathajzer told him that the Germans had been waiting when the two arrived. They had killed the rescuers as well as the small group of people the men led out. The Nazis had been alerted to the Jewish rescue endeavor by a woman who thought she had seen a group of Jews leave the sewer that morning. Annoyed that the first group had slipped from their grasp, the Germans decided to lay an ambush for any further rescue parties. While Rathajzer had earlier been thrilled with the day's events, now he was filled with a deep sense of sorrow.

What remained of the ghetto after the uprising
was soon destroyed by Stroop's army.

The Rebellion's End

The Jewish rebellion lasted for about 28 days, but even afterward the Nazis continued to scour the ghetto for any bunkers they might have overlooked. Here and there, small pockets of Jews were rounded up and either immediately executed or sent off on transports. On May 16, General Stroop finally signaled the end of Warsaw's Jews with a symbolic gesture to please his superiors. He blew up Warsaw's magnificent Jewish synagogue, which had been built in 1877 by the famous architect Leonard Marconi.

Stroop made certain that he alone pressed the detonator reducing the splendid structure to rubble, since the general wished to be assured a place in Nazi history. As the synagogue exploded, Stroop shouted "Heil Hitler!" and thought about how the führer would have enjoyed this sight. Later that evening, he sent the SS high command a cable that read, "The former Jewish quarter of Warsaw no longer exists."

Yet there are those who would disagree with Stroop's appraisal of the situation. Although Warsaw's ghetto was physically demolished, the indestructible spirits and courage of its rebels became legendary. Their heroic actions in the face of overwhelming odds have remained inspirational to oppressed people through the years. Perhaps the Warsaw ghetto will continue to exist for as long as we remember those who fought to preserve it.

Major General Jürgen Stroop was awarded the Iron Cross, First Class, for his handling of the Warsaw ghetto. From September to November 1943 Stroop served in the highly desirable post of SS and police commander in Greece. On July 18, 1951, the former Nazi general stood trial in Poland for war crimes and was sentenced to death. To the very end, he remained arrogant and unrepentant, blaming any wrongdoings on his subordinates. Jürgen Stroop was hanged in Warsaw on March 6, 1952.

Yitzhak Zuckerman and Ziuvia Lubetkin settled in Palestine (which became Israel in 1948) following the war. There the couple began a kibbutz (farm collective) called Kibbutz Lochamai Hagetaot (Ghetto Fighters' Kibbutz). Later on, Yitzhak Zuckerman ran an international documentation center on the European ghettos.

Simcha Rathajzer moved to Palestine, too, where he became a successful businessman.

Marek Edelman, who shared the ZOB command with Ziuvia Lubetkin in the last days of the rebellion, remained in Poland following the war and later became an outstanding heart specialist. Decades after the rebellion, Edelman once again opposed an oppressive regime. This time he actively supported Solidarity, an organization made up of 50 Polish trade unions. Regarded with hostility by the Polish Communist government, Solidarity was outlawed in 1982, when hundreds of labor union leaders were imprisoned. However, over the next few years they were released and in 1989 the ban on Solidarity was lifted.

Captain Henryk Iwanski of the Polish Home Army continued to conduct ghetto rescue missions until he was severely wounded by the Nazis in 1943. After the war, Poland's Communist government arrested him, along with other Home Army officers, and imprisoned him for seven years. Following his release, Iwanski, who still suffered from his war injuries, lived in Poland with his wife in near poverty.

Labor camp workers—the Warsaw Jews sent to labor camps, where the German factories had been relocated—largely remained there until November 1943. Then most were taken out to the large ditches they had previously been told to dig as protection against air raids, and were shot. The workers' bodies were heaped on top of one another in these mass graves.

SOURCE NOTES

Prologue

1. V. L. Benes and N. J. G. Pounds, *Poland* (New York: Prager, 1970), p. 106.
2. Hanna Krall, *Shielding the Flame: An Intimate Conversation with Dr. Marek Edelman, the Last Surviving Leader of the Warsaw Ghetto Uprising* (New York: Holt, 1986), p. 122.

Chapter 1

1. Abraham I. Katsh, ed. and trans., *Scroll of Agony: The Warsaw Ghetto Diary of Chaim A. Kamlan* (New York: Macmillan, 1965), p. 274.
2. Interview with Eva Kampinski, Video Archives for Holocaust Testimonies/Holocaust Resource Center of Kean College.

Chapter 2

1. Dan Kurzman, *The Bravest Battle: The Twenty-eight Days of the Warsaw Ghetto Uprising* (New York: G.P. Putnam's Sons, 1976), p. 37.

Chapter 3

1. Raul Hilberg, Stanislaw Staron, and Josef Kermisz, eds., *The Warsaw Diary of Adam Czerniakow: Prelude to Doom* (New York: Stein and Day, 1979), p. 111.

Chapter 6

1. Dan Kurzman, *The Bravest Battle: The Twenty-eight Days of the Warsaw Ghetto Uprising* (New York: G. P. Putnam's Sons, 1976), p. 176.

Chapter 8

1. Dan Kurzman, *The Bravest Battle: The Twenty-eight Days of the Warsaw Ghetto Uprising* (New York: G. P. Putnam's Sons, 1976), p. 257.

Chapter 9

1. Jürgen Stroop, *The Stroop Report* (New York: Random House, 1979), p. 53.

For Further Reading

Bartov, Omer. *Hitler's Army: Soldiers, Nazis, and the War in the Third Reich*. New York: Oxford University Press, 1991.

Bialoszewski, Miron. *A Memoir of the Warsaw Uprising*. Ann Arbor, Michigan: Ardis, 1977.

Browning, Christopher R. *Ordinary Men: Reserve Police Battalion 101 and the Final Solution in Poland*. New York: HarperCollins, 1992.

Frank, Anne. *The Works of Anne Frank*. Westport, Connecticut: Greenwood, 1974.

Friedman, Ina R. *The Other Victims: First-Person Stories of Non-Jews Persecuted by the Nazis*. Boston: Houghton Mifflin, 1990.

Kunhardt, Philip B. *Life: World War II*. Boston: Little, Brown, 1990.

Landau, Elaine. *Nazi War Criminals*. New York: Franklin Watts, 1990.

Landau, Elaine. *We Survived the Holocaust*. New York: Franklin Watts, 1991.

Miller, Judith. *One, By One, By One*. New York: Simon and Schuster, 1990.

Salsitz, Norman, and Amalie Peteanker Salsitz. *Against All Odds*. New York: Holocaust Publications, 1991.

Sloan, Jacob, trans. *From the Warsaw Ghetto: The Journal of Emmanuel Ringelblum*. New York: Schocken Books, 1958.

Szwajger, Adina Blady. *I Remember Nothing More: The Warsaw Children's Hospital and the Jewish Resistance*. New York: Pantheon, 1991.

INDEX

Allied forces, 32
Anielewicz, Mordechai, 25-27, 37-39, 50-53, 77, 84, 86, 91, 97, 101, 106, 109, 111, 119-124
Anti-Fascist Bloc, 25, 26
Appelbojm, David, 39, 101, 104
Artsein, Zachariah, 27, 28
attic passages, 58, 59, 69

barter system, 12
black market, 34
Blosche, Josef, 15
Brandt, First Lieutenant Karl, 50
bribes, 60, 62
Bund (Hebrew Social Democratic Party), 25
bunkers, 28, 29, 49, 71, 72, 76, 82, 84, 93, 100, 111, 112

Church of the Virgin Mary, 60
Czerniakow, Adam, 41

Dehmke, Otto, 81
deportation, 17-20, 33, 42, 64, 74
    children, 19

Edelman, Marek, 123, 124, 129, 134
employment cards, 17
extermination centers, 6, 42, 43, 60, 74

flags, 63, 69, 79
Frank, Hans, 72, 73
Fuden, Regina, 87, 88, 104

ghetto police, 20, 22, 99, 100
ghettos, 6

Himmler, Heinrich, 45, 46, 73, 74, 87
Hitler, Adolf, 5, 49, 73
Home Army (Armia Krajowa), 31, 32, 38-41, 51, 60, 63, 87, 102, 103, 115, 119

informers, 28, 34, 45, 84, 109
Iwanski, Captain Henryk, 39, 102-104, 115-117, 135

Jewish Fighting Organization (Zydowska Orgawizacja Bojowa), see ZOB
Jewish Military Organization, see ZZW
"Jewish question," the, 6
Jews, 6
Judenrat, 10, 39-42, 50, 51, 82

Kibbutz Lochamai Hagetaot, 134
Klaustermeyer, Heinrich, 15
Korczak, Janusz, 19

labor camps, 6, 16
Lichtenbaum, Marek, 41, 42
Lubetkin, Ziuvia, 37, 39, 92, 94, 97, 120, 123-126, 128, 129, 134

Marconi, Leonard, 133

Nazis, 5, 6

Palestine, 134
Passover, 49, 50
Pawaik Prison, 96
poison, 81, 82
Polish flag, 63, 69, 79
Polish underground, 39, 55, 102, 107
Polish Workers' Party (PPR), 25, 26

Rathajzer, Simcha, 124-131, 134

seder, 49
sewers, 115, 124, 127-131
Skosowski, Leon, 44, 45
slave labor, 44
smugglers, 12, 13, 22, 84, 120
snipers, 70, 71
Solidarity, 134

Stroop, Major General Jurgen, 45-48, 52, 53, 56-65, 67, 70, 73, 74, 79-81, 86, 87, 93-95, 99, 103, 110-116, 133, 134
suicide, 81, 82, 122, 123
Szerynski, Joseph, 20, 22

tunnels, 41, 83, 94, 95, 101-104, 115-117, 124, 127-131

Ukrainian soldiers, 52, 54, 55

von Sammern-Frankenegg, Colonel Ferdinand, 45, 52-57

Warsaw, 5, 73
gentile district, 33, 37, 41, 65, 83, 84-86, 94, 103, 119, 126
Warsaw ghetto, 9
brush factory district, 10, 42-44, 68, 71, 72, 77, 79, 114
burning of, 76, 77, 91-95, 114
central ghetto, 10, 77, 93, 111
conditions in, 10, 11
cultural life in, 15
education in, 15
illegal residents, 22
productive ghetto, 9, 63, 93
starvation in, 16
"wild" ghetto, 22
Warsaw synagogue, 133
Wilner, Arie, 29-35

Zegota (Council for Aid to the Jews), 33
Zionist flag, 63, 69, 79
ZOB, 25, 26, 37-44, 52, 63, 65, 75-77, 88, 100, 101, 104, 105, 123
Zuckerman, Yitzhak, 37-39, 86, 97, 119, 120, 128, 134
ZZW, 39-41, 45, 52, 69, 77, 79-82, 115-117

Elaine Landau received a bachelor's degree from New York University and a master's degree in library and information science from Pratt Institute. She has worked as a newspaper reporter, an editor, and a youth services librarian, but especially enjoys writing for young people.

Ms. Landau has published more than fifty books, including *Nazi War Criminals* and *We Survived the Holocaust*.

Southern Sr. High Media Center
Harwood, Maryland 20776